Other books by Annette Annechild:

Getting into Your Wok with Annette Annechild

Recipe for a Great Affair (with Russell Bennett)

Annette Annechild's Wok Your Way Skinny

Falling in Love with Your FOOD PROCESSOR

by Annette Annechild

Food Consultant: Skip Skwarek

A WALLABY BOOK

Published by Simon & Schuster • New York

Copyright © 1983 by Annette Annechild
All rights reserved
including the right of reproduction
in whole or in part in any form
Published by Wallaby Books
A Simon & Schuster Division of Gulf & Western Corporation
Simon & Schuster Building
1230 Avenue of the Americas
New York, New York 10020

Designed by Irving Perkins Associates
WALLABY and colophon are registered trademarks of Simon & Schuster
First Wallaby Books printing June 1983
10 9 8 7 6 5 4 3 2 1
Manufactured in the United States of America
Printed and bound by Command Web

Library of Congress Cataloging in Publication Data

Annechild, Annette.
  Falling in Love with Your Food Processor
  "A Wallaby book."
  Includes index.
  1. Food processor cookery.   I. Skwarek, Skip.
II. Title.   III. Title: Falling in Love with Your Food Processor.
TX840.F6A56   1983   641.5'89   82-25602
ISBN: 0-671-45391-2

*This book is dedicated to
the memory of my grandmother,
Lucia Anastasio,
and to her three daughters,
Anne, Jean and Mary,
all of whom taught me
that food, like love, should be
healthy, beautiful and abundant*

ACKNOWLEDGMENTS

With special thanks to John Boswell for his inspiration and advice; Patti Brown for her enthusiasm and creative support; Gene Brissie, Debra Downing and Jack Artenstein of Simon & Schuster for their belief and guidance; Ed and Eileen Friedman for their constant encouragement and professional assistance; Michael Goodman for his helpful introductions; Melodie Woods Celecia, Bob Celecia, Linda Chenault, Stanley Goodman, Raymond Heremaia and Allen Balderson for their creative California contributions; Linda West and Charles Stetler for making testing and tasting so much fun; my talented recipe contributors, Russell Bennett, Ada Chiofalo, Judy and Jim Glenn, Cristina Eisenberg, Aunt Jean, and especially my parents, Anne and Frank Viscardi; Laura Bialosky, Jimmy Glenn and Christopher Brenner for living in the craziness of a cookbook writer's life with so much love and laughter; Linda Chambers, for assisting me as typographer, cohort and friend in yet another venture; Barbara, Bob and Leonora Tint for their years of family feelings; and with the greatest appreciation to Skip Skwarek, a food consultant and top New York chef in his own right, who shared his home, his ideas and expertise, and endless hours seated beside me developing this book. I love you all.

The recipes in this book were tested on a Cuisinart DLC-7 food processor as well as on several other machines. The author wishes to thank Karl Sondheimer and Cuisinart, Inc., for generously supplying their product.

"THE NATURAL ORDER OF THINGS"

INTRODUCTION

In the sixties, Americans were introduced to the concept of "health food" in response to the overwhelming diet of "junk food" to which we had become accustomed. Health food stores sprang up all over the country stocked with beans, grains, seeds and a variety of new products that very few of us really knew what to do with. Unfortunately, the fare produced with these ingredients was often heavy and unappetizing and the fact that it was good for us just wasn't enough. Having grown up in an old-fashioned Italian household, I recognized some of these "new" products, like lentils and grains, and better yet, I still remembered what my grandmother used to do with them! Some of the products *were* new, like tofu and miso paste, and it took years of experimenting to understand their potential.

Now, twenty years later, "health food" has become "natural food" and America's awakened interest in diet and nutrition has brought with it a renewed interest in a more aware and natural cuisine. My direction in the food field has been to incorporate the techniques of all the great cuisines with natural, healthy ingredients.

I believe food can be delicious, beautiful, healthy and naturally slenderizing as well. Looking back, I realize "health food" wasn't ever really *new* —it was the country cooking of past generations introduced to an America that had become used to overly treated, rich foods and all-too-available junk-food treats.

All of my books for the "new age kitchen" are designed to implement the fast, fun appliances available in the eighties to create a wholesome, money-saving, great-tasting cuisine—fast food that will both excite your tastebuds and nourish your body. I believe no single appliance has ever increased the potential of our kitchens more than the food processor. It can make an inexperienced cook feel like a gourmet chef overnight—it's that fast and easy. With this book and your processor, you can turn your kitchen into a pantry filled with delicious natural goodies.

The first chapter acquaints the beginner with everything this amazing machine can do with a simple step-by-step plan. The second centers on how to stock your kitchen in one afternoon with natural staples that will save you time and money. After that, you're on your way with a collection of recipes that includes appetizers, breakfast, lunch, dinner and dessert.

I truly believe that this is food for the eighties—fast, fun, easy and great for you, too!

All the best,

Annette Annechild

Annette Annechild

Falling in Love with Your FOOD PROCESSOR

Chapter 1

HOW TO HAVE FUN WITH YOUR FOOD PROCESSOR

The first step in having fun with your food processor is understanding it completely. Once you have read your instruction booklet carefully, you are ready to learn exactly what your food processor can do. By mastering the basic techniques of food processor cookery, any apprehensions you might have about this incredible machine will vanish and the fun will really start! Remember that all machines are different. We have tried to keep our instructions and recipes general enough to be easily adaptable to most machines. In all my books, my aim is to keep everything as easy and simple as possible, probably because I hate complicated directions when I am trying to learn something new. With this in mind, we have designed a *four lesson plan* that will acquaint you step-by-step with all the basic techniques, as well as give you great things to eat! We recommend setting aside one afternoon and going through all the lessons at one time. A total grocery list for all four lessons is included as well as an individual ingredient list for each of the separate lessons.

We have chosen to take you through many of the basic techniques using one vegetable processed different ways—so grab a bunch of carrots and come along. . . .

THE BASICS

Your machine comes with a *food pusher*, a *work bowl* and a *cover* equipped with a *feed tube* (either regular or expanded in size).

Standard equipment also includes a number of varieties of *blades* and *discs*. Usually, four are provided with your machine.

They are:

1. **The steel blade.** The "workhorse" that *chops, grinds, purées, mixes, grates* and even *kneads* dough.
2. **The metal slicing disc.** This disc actually *slices* ingredients either thick or thin, the size of the slices being somewhat controlled by the amount of pressure you apply to the food pusher. Lighter pressure—thinner slices. (There are also optional slicing discs available that give thinner or thicker slices.)
3. **The metal shredding disc.** This disc yields short or long *shreds*.
4. **The plastic blade.** This blade is used for *mixing* batters and *kneading* doughs.

FOOD PROCESSOR DO'S AND DON'TS

Never:

1. Place your fingers or anything other than food or the food pusher into feed tube with machine running.
2. Fill the work bowl beyond capacity recommended in your instruction booklet.
3. Remove cover without blade having *completely* stopped.
4. Attempt to process anything not recommended for your machine.
5. Use blades not designed for your machine.
6. Put blades on shaft without bowl being locked in place.
7. Attempt to grind grain or coffee beans, slice solidly frozen food or process any food too hard for the tip of a sharp knife to be inserted into easily.

Always:

1. Clean machine carefully after using and dry well.
2. Keep your processor *unplugged* when not in use.
3. Use the food pusher.

4. Have cover locked in place before turning on.
5. Handle the blades carefully.
6. Remove bowl and blade or disc according to instruction booklet.
7. Process dry ingredients before wet ones to save having to clean bowl often.

MENU FOR THE FOUR LESSON PLAN

CARROT ORANGE COTTAGE SNACK
SPINACH PESTO SAUCE FOR PASTA
MARINATED FRESH VEGETABLE SALAD
APPLE CARROT MUFFINS

Total Grocery List for the Four Lesson Plan

    1 bunch carrots
   ¼ cup orange juice
    2 large lettuce leaves
   ½ cup large curd cottage cheese
    2 small bunches parsley
   ¼ pound Parmesan cheese in 1 piece
   ½ cup hulled sunflower seeds
    1 pound fresh spinach leaves
    1 tablespoon dried basil
   ¾ teaspoon salt
  1¼ teaspoon black pepper
    2 large cloves garlic
  1⅔ cups olive oil
   ½ pound fresh green beans
   ¼ pound mushrooms
    1 onion
   ½ teaspoon oregano
   ½ teaspoon tarragon
   ⅓ cup apple cider vinegar
    1 apple
  1½ cups unbleached white flour
   ½ teaspoon cinnamon
    1 teaspoon baking powder
    1 teaspoon baking soda
   ¾ cup butter
   ½ cup brown sugar
    1 egg
    1 teaspoon lemon juice
    2 tablespoons shortening

Each lesson covers a different blade. For the first part of Lesson I, in which you will make a carrot-orange-cottage cheese snack, you will need:

2 carrots (scrubbed)
¼ cup orange juice
½ cup large curd cottage cheese
2 large lettuce leaves
1 sprig parsley

To see what this blade actually does, begin by:

1. Setting up your machine according to your instruction booklet.
2. Take 2 carrots, scrub and cut into 2-inch lengths.
3. Insert the *steel blade*.
4. Place cut up carrots in work bowl. Cover bowl according to instructions.
5. Start machine and count to 5 slowly (5 seconds). Stop machine, look in work bowl and scrape down sides of work bowl with a spatula. These are *coarsely chopped* carrots.
6. Replace cover.
7. Start machine again to repeat processing for another 5 seconds.
8. Stop machine. Scrape down sides and observe *finely chopped* carrots.
9. Put cover back on.
10. Start machine. Repeat for a third time, processing for 15 seconds.
11. Stop machine, scrape down sides and observe *finely minced* carrots.
12. Add orange juice. Cover, turn machine back on and process until puréed, about 45 seconds.
13. Stop machine, add cottage cheese. Process in several on/off bursts just to combine.
14. Place lettuce leaves on plate. Spoon mixture into center. Garnish with parsley.
15. Sit down and enjoy a healthy snack!

Break's over! Now back to the second half of Lesson I:

Variations with the Steel Blade

To demonstrate the many variations for which you can use the steel blade, you will be making Spinach Pesto Sauce—either for tonight's dinner or easily frozen for later use.
You will need:

¼ pound Parmesan cheese in 1 piece
½ cup hulled sunflower seeds
1 pound fresh spinach leaves (stems removed, washed and drained well)
1 small bunch parsley (stems removed, washed and drained well)

1 tablespoon dried basil
½ teaspoon salt
1 teaspoon black pepper
2 large cloves garlic (peeled)
1 cup olive oil

1. Wash work bowl and blade. Dry well.
2. Cut rind off cheese and cut into 1-inch pieces.
3. Insert *steel blade* and, with work bowl in place, place cheese cubes in bowl and cover.
4. Turn on machine and process 40–60 seconds or until *finely grated.*
5. Remove cheese from bowl and set aside.
6. Replace bowl and blade and add sunflower seeds to bowl. Cover and process 30 seconds or until *finely chopped.*
7. Remove cover and add spinach leaves, parsley, basil, salt, pepper and grated cheese. Cover.
8. Start machine, drop garlic cloves down feed tube and slowly add oil through feed tube, with machine running. Process until smooth and thick (about 1 minute total time).
9. Take cover off and taste. More garlic or salt and pepper can be added to suit your taste by just adding them to work bowl and processing further.
10. With machine off, remove cover, remove work bowl and blade from machine, pour sauce into container with cover. Can be refrigerated for several days or frozen for later use. To use, simply pour over freshly cooked, drained pasta.

Congratulations! Now you can proceed to Lesson II. . . .

LESSON II **THE SLICING DISC**

Back to the trusty carrot once again. To demonstrate the slicing disc, you will be making Marinated Fresh Vegetable Salad.
You will need:

3 carrots (scrubbed, left whole and trimmed to height of your feed tube)
½ pound fresh green beans
¼ pound mushrooms (brushed or wiped with paper towel)
1 whole onion (size chosen to fit your feed tube *whole*)
1 small bunch parsley (stems removed, rinsed and dried)
½ teaspoon oregano
½ teaspoon tarragon
¼ teaspoon salt
¼ teaspoon black pepper
⅓ cup apple cider vinegar
⅔ cup olive oil

1. Clean machine and insert *slicing disc.*
2. Place cover on machine.
3. Place carrots standing straight up in feed tube—as many as will fit snugly in the feed tube.
4. Hold food pusher on top of carrots with light pressure.
5. Turn machine on and press lightly with food pusher until half the length of the carrots has been sliced.
6. Turn machine off. Be sure to wait until disc stops spinning. Remove cover and *slicing disc* and look at thickness of slices. They will be *thinly sliced.* If they have come out unevenly sliced, it is probably because the feed tube was not packed tightly enough. You want to pack the feed tube tightly to insure uniform slices.
7. Leave sliced carrots in work bowl and replace *slicing disc.*
8. Replace cover, repack feed tube with unsliced portion of carrots.
9. Insert food pusher in feed tube, this time use *firm pressure.*
10. Turn machine on and with *firm pressure* push carrots through.
11. Stop machine. Remove cover. Note different thickness of slices. *Firm pressure* yields *thicker slices* on hard foods like carrots.
12. Remove *slicing disc* and empty carrots into large glass, ceramic or stainless steel bowl.
13. Replace work bowl and *slicing disc* on machine.
14. Measure remaining carrot pieces to bottom of feed tube and cut them to fit when packed *horizontally* into feed tube.
15. Replace cover. Insert food pusher. Start machine, start with *light pressure* and continue with *firm pressure* on the food pusher.
16. Turn machine off. Remove cover and *slicing disc* and observe the long, attractive carrot slices. Remove to bowl with other carrots.
17. Now here come the green beans! Rinse beans and drain. Snap off stem at top (if any) and pull down to remove string. Trim the green beans to fit horizontally in feed tube.
18. Replace work bowl, *slicing disc* and cover.
19. Pack feed tube horizontally three-quarters full with green beans.
20. Insert the food pusher and with *light pressure* turn machine on and maintain *light pressure* until all beans have been sliced.
21. Turn machine off. Remove cover and slicing disc and observe french cut green beans!
22. You can leave processed beans in work bowl. Replace disc and cover, and repeat until all beans are similarly processed. Remove and add to carrots in bowl.
23. Next are the mushrooms. Have work bowl and *slicing disc* in place. Pack feed tube with mushrooms horizontally placed stem to stem, caps facing out. Pack tightly.
24. Insert food pusher. Maintain *light pressure.* Turn machine on. Repeat until all mushrooms are sliced. Remove cover and disc and remove mushrooms to bowl.
25. Peel onion and slice off root end with knife.
26. Replace work bowl, *slicing disc* and cover.
27. Place onion in feed tube with root end *down* (toward blade). (If onion is too large, cut in half through root end, place half in feed tube root end down. Process each half as follows.)

28. Turn machine on and process with *light pressure* on food pusher. This will yield pretty onion rings (or half slices). Turn off machine, remove disc and add onions to bowl.
29. Replace work bowl and now, to refresh Lesson I, insert *steel blade*.
30. Add parsley, oregano, tarragon, salt, pepper and vinegar. Cover and turn on machine. Process 5 seconds.
31. Slowly pour olive oil into feed tube with machine running, process 20 seconds or until mixture is well combined and parsley is finely chopped.
32. Turn off machine. Remove cover. Remove work bowl from machine and blade from work bowl. Pour contents of work bowl over vegetables. Toss well. Cover and marinate for several hours in refrigerator, or overnight.

You have now mastered several uses of the *steel blade* and variations with the *slicing disc*. You also have prepared a delicious marinated salad.

The *slicing disc* can also be used for raw meat that has been partially frozen, cold cooked meat, cold soft or semi-soft cheeses, bread and a great variety of fruits and vegetables. Try your hand at a cored apple, an orange or a tomato as soon as possible. If you have a small feed tube, simply trim ingredients to proper size. An expanded feed tube can even handle a loaf of french bread easily.

LESSON III THE SHREDDING DISC

Lessons III and IV combine to create tasty Apple Carrot Muffins. You'll be amazed at how fast baking can be with your food processor.
You will need for both lessons:

    2 large carrots (scrubbed)
    1 apple (cored)
    1½ cups unbleached white flour
    ½ teaspoon cinnamon
    1 teaspoon baking powder
    1 teaspoon baking soda
    ¼ teaspoon salt
    ¾ cup butter at room temperature
    ½ cup brown sugar
    1 egg
    1 teaspoon lemon juice
    1 tablespoon water
      A 12-cup muffin pan
    2 tablespoons shortening for greasing muffin pan

1. Clean work bowl and blades. Replace work bowl and insert *shredding disc*.

2. To get used to packing feed tube both vertically and horizontally, you will use both methods here.
3. Cut one carrot into pieces that fit horizontally into bottom of your feed tube.
4. Replace cover and with *medium pressure* on food pusher, turn machine on and process until carrots are shredded.
5. Turn off machine. Remove cover and *shredding disc;* note the long, slender shreds. Remove 12 of them and set aside, covered.
6. Replace *shredding disc* and cover. Pack feed tube to top with second carrot vertically, trimmed to fit the length of feed tube to within ¼-inch.
7. Insert food pusher, exert *medium pressure*. Turn machine on and process until carrots are shredded. Note that the shreds are shorter with vertical packing.
8. Turn machine off, remove food pusher. If your feed tube is large enough, insert whole apple from bottom; otherwise, quarter and pack feed tube from top.
9. Insert food pusher; exert *medium pressure*. Turn machine on and process until shredded.
10. Turn off machine. Remove cover and *shredding disc*. Remove carrots and apple from work bowl and place in bowl. Sprinkle with lemon juice. Set aside.

Continue to Lesson IV. . . .

LESSON IV **THE PLASTIC BLADE**

The second part of this recipe uses the plastic blade . . . and requires a clean, dry work bowl.

1. With *plastic blade* in place, add flour, cinnamon, baking powder, baking soda and salt to work bowl. Process 4–5 1-second bursts to sift and combine. Remove to small bowl and set aside.
2. With *plastic blade* still in place, add butter to work bowl. Cover, turn machine on and process 45 seconds.
3. With machine running, add brown sugar 1 tablespoon at a time. Continue processing until butter and sugar are light and fluffy.
4. With machine running, break egg into feed tube and process 30 seconds. Turn machine off.
5. Remove cover, add dry ingredients all at once to work bowl.
6. Replace cover. Turn machine on and process 10 seconds or just until blended. Turn off machine and remove cover. Add 1 tablespoon water.
7. Add shredded carrots and apple. Replace cover and turn machine on; process 5 seconds just to combine. Stop processor. Remove cover and

spoon batter into 12 greased muffin cups, until two-thirds full. Take reserved carrot strands and place one on each muffin in circular shape.
8. Bake at 350° for 35 minutes or until golden.

Well, you did it! In four easy lessons, you have mastered basic techniques for the four essential discs and blades and have produced a carrot orange cottage snack, a pesto sauce for pasta, a marinated salad and dessert! Congratulations—the fun is just beginning. . . .

Chapter 2

STOCKING YOUR KITCHEN WITH NATURAL FOOD PROCESSOR GOODIES

Once you own a food processor, you can have goodies on hand such as your own homemade mayonnaise, peanut butter, salad dressing, cheese dips and bread crumbs—to name just a few.

This chapter is devoted to recipes for all the basics. In one afternoon you can stock your cupboard, refrigerator and freezer with homemade staples that will save you money and insure the highest nutritional content possible with no preservatives added.

Cristina's Mayonnaise

Within this book you will discover many recipes created by Cristina Eisenberg. I met Cristina and her husband Steve through my great friends, Ed and Eileen Friedman. They have a beautiful home in Venice, California, with a great kitchen that Cristina lives in—much to Steve's delight. Cristina offered her assistance in my book building and her efforts are a special treat for all of us. Thanks, Cristina!

Ingredients:

1 whole large egg plus 1 egg yolk
½ teaspoon salt
½ teaspoon Dijon mustard
Dash Tabasco sauce
½ tablespoon lemon juice
Dash Worcestershire sauce
1 cup safflower oil
½ cup peanut oil

1. With steel blade in place, place eggs, salt, mustard, Tabasco sauce, lemon juice and Worcestershire sauce into bowl of processor. Process until well blended, about 3 seconds.
2. With processor still running, pour in the oils very slowly. When you finish pouring in the oils, the eggs will have become emulsified and you will have 1½ cups mayonnaise.
3. To store, refrigerate in a tightly covered plastic container.

YIELD: *1½ cups*

Tofu "Mayonnaise"

This one is a "must try." It's high protein, low calorie, eggless "mayonnaise" that tastes so good you may never make the regular kind again!

Ingredients:

1 pound tofu (drained 15 minutes and squeezed—the more moisture you press or squeeze from the tofu the thicker the dressing will be)

⅓ cup lemon juice, or more to thin dressing

2 teaspoons Dijon-style mustard

¼ teaspoon hot chili oil

¼ cup olive oil (optional: if you're watching calories closely you can omit the oil and it still tastes great)

1. With steel blade in place, crumble tofu into work bowl. Cover and process until completely smooth.
2. Scrape down sides of work bowl. Add lemon juice, mustard and chili oil. Process 10 seconds or until well combined.
3. Add olive oil if desired. (It will give the dressing a bit more of a satiny texture plus the distinctive flavor of the oil.) Process 10 seconds.
4. Spoon into pint container and store tightly covered in the refrigerator.

YIELD: *2 cups*

Variations (the following suggestions also apply to Cristina's Mayonnaise on previous page):

1. *The simplest variation.* Substitute rice wine vinegar or a vinegar of your choice for the lemon juice, or use lime instead of lemon to give the dressing a special tang that goes well with salads containing fruit.
2. *Herb.* Add ¼ cup fresh (or 2 teaspoons dried) dill, basil, parsley, tarragon or chervil when adding the lemon juice. Be creative and combine several of your favorite herbs to come up with your own "house" dressing. This and the following variations are best made several hours or a day in advance to allow the flavor to develop.
3. *Spinach.* Add ½ cup blanched, drained and squeezed spinach to the work bowl with the crumbled tofu. Add ¼ teaspoon freshly grated nutmeg with the lemon juice. Excellent on cold poached fish.
4. *Garlic.* Add 4 large, peeled cloves and a 1-inch piece of peeled ginger root to the work bowl with the crumbled tofu. A tasty dip for fresh vegetables.
5. *Blue cheese.* If you like it smooth and creamy, add 2 ounces blue cheese or Gorgonzola to work bowl with the crumbled tofu. If you prefer it on the chunky side, add the cheese after all basic ingredients are smooth and process briefly just to crumble cheese and distribute throughout the dressing. Try this over poached pears for an outstanding dessert.

Homemade Horseradish

Ingredients:

¼ pound fresh horseradish root
(scrubbed and scraped)
White wine or cider vinegar

Coarse salt (optional)
Caraway seeds (optional)

1. With shredding disc in place, load scraped horseradish roots vertically in feed tube.
2. Keeping firm pressure on food pusher, start processor and shred roots.
3. Remove grated root to small bowl and mix in enough vinegar to moisten thoroughly.
4. If desired, add approximately ½ teaspoon coarse salt and ¼ teaspoon caraway seeds to taste.
5. Transfer to glass jar with tight-fitting lid. Keeps indefinitely in refrigerator, although it will tend to lose its potency and taste more like the commercial preparation after 4 or 5 weeks.

YIELD: ¾ *cup*

Simple Garlic Vinaigrette

Ingredients:

2 large cloves garlic (peeled)
⅔ cup white wine or cider vinegar
1 tablespoon tamari (soy sauce)
1 tablespoon Dijon-style mustard
1⅓ cups safflower or sunflower oil
½ teaspoon hot chili oil

1. With steel blade in place, lock cover in place. Turn processor on and drop garlic cloves into feed tube. Process 3 seconds or until finely minced. Stop processor, remove cover and scrape down sides of work bowl with spatula.
2. Add vinegar, tamari and mustard. Lock cover in place. Stir chili oil into safflower or sunflower oil.
3. Turn processor on. Slowly pour oil down feed tube, adding all oil within 30 seconds. Process 5 seconds more. Stop processor. Remove cover. Remove work bowl from motor. Remove steel blade from bowl. Pour dressing into pint jar and store tightly covered in refrigerator.

YIELD: *2 cups*

NOTE: Flavor may be varied by using different vinegar or substituting lemon juice for part or all of the vinegar. Likewise, peanut, corn or olive oil will add different nuances. Experiment and come up with a mixture that suits your palate.

Blanche Flotsambottom's Sweet and Sour Celery Seed Salad Dressing

Particularly good with salads containing fruit.

Ingredients:

1 small onion (peeled, root end trimmed and quartered)
2 large cloves garlic (peeled)
½ cup red wine vinegar
⅓ cup raw honey
2 teaspoons celery seed

1 teaspoon tarragon leaves
1 teaspoon dry mustard
1 teaspoon salt
1 teaspoon freshly ground pepper
1 cup olive oil

1. With steel blade in place, add onion to work bowl. Lock cover in place and start processor. Drop garlic cloves through feed tube. Process 5 seconds.
2. Stop processor, remove cover and scrape down sides of work bowl with spatula. Add remaining ingredients except oil.
3. Lock cover in place and start processor. Slowly add oil through feed tube, taking about 20 seconds. Process 5 seconds longer after all oil is added.
4. Stop processor. Remove cover. Remove work bowl from base. Remove steel blade from work bowl and pour contents into pint container. This can be stored covered in refrigerator for up to 1 week. Shake well before using. Serve at room temperature.

YIELD: *2 cups*

Traditional Pesto Sauce

Ingredients:

6 cups fresh basil leaves (tightly packed, washed and dried)
1 bunch Italian parsley (rinsed, dried and stems removed)
2 teaspoons pepper

6 cloves garlic peeled
¾ cup pignoli nuts or walnuts
¾ cup grated Parmesan cheese
1 cup olive oil

1. With steel blade in place, add basil, parsley, pepper, garlic, nuts and cheese to work bowl. Cover and process until fairly smooth.
2. With machine running, pour oil in slowly through feed tube. Process until well combined.
3. Serve over hot pasta. Generally ½ cup pesto is used for ½ pound pasta. One-quarter cup of hot water can be added to the pesto sauce, which both warms and thins the sauce.

YIELD: *2½ cups*

NOTE: To store pesto, place in a jar and cover with ½-inch olive oil. Cover tightly and store in the refrigerator.

Homemade Tahini

Tahini is great in sauces, spread on whole grain bread or used as a dip for vegetables. You can make it to desired consistency by the amount of oil you choose to use.

Ingredients:

1 cup sesame paste (available in natural food stores)

3 cloves garlic (peeled)
Juice of 1 lemon
Olive oil

1. With steel blade in place, add sesame paste to work bowl. Cover and start processor. Immediately drop garlic down feed tube.
2. Pour lemon juice through feed tube.
3. Pour olive oil in until desired consistency is reached.
4. Store in a jar in the refrigerator.

YIELD: *1 cup*

FLAVORED BUTTERS

Garlic, olives, anchovies, dill and parsley all lend an incredible flavor to butter.

Simply process flavoring ingredient first with steel blade. Peeled garlic cloves and pitted olives should be added through the feed tube with the motor running; anchovies, dill, and parsley may be added directly to the work bowl. Process until finely minced. Add butter, at room temperature, in 1-inch pieces. Process until creamy and well combined.

Flavored butters may be stored, covered, in the refrigerator for up to one week, or wrapped airtight and frozen for up to two months.

For those of you who have never tried flavored butters, here are some guidelines per half-pound of unsalted butter:

Garlic. Use 3–4 cloves.

Olive. Use 4–6 stuffed green or ripe Greek olives.

Anchovy. Use 4 anchovy fillets and ⅛ teaspoon hot pepper sauce.

Herb. Use ¼ cup fresh herbs or 2 teaspoons dried.

Do remember that you can adjust these amounts to suit your taste. Scallions, shallots, ginger root, citrus zest, capers, horseradish, and grated sharp-flavored cheeses are also candidates for flavoring butters. Use individually or combine to create your own special touch of flavor-enhancing elegance.

PEANUT BUTTER

Using steel blade, process 2–3 cups of peanuts at one time. Let the machine run continuously. After 2 or 3 minutes, ground nuts will form a ball, which then will slowly disappear. Scrape down sides and continue processing until desired smoothness is obtained. For chunky peanut butter, add ½–1 cup whole peanuts as soon as ball begins to disappear.

Store in covered jar in refrigerator.

NOTE: See chapter 5 for many more ideas with ground nut butters.

CHOPPED NUTS

Nuts are an excellent source of protein and add a wonderful, crunchy texture to many dishes. Walnuts and cashews are especially versatile nuts to have on hand.

The shredding disc will process nuts to a fine uniform texture but not as finely as the steel blade.

You can chop up to 2 cups of nuts at a time, checking frequently for desired texture. Pack processed nuts into airtight containers or bags, label and freeze for later use.

FLAVORING YOUR OWN YOGURT

Unfortunately, most flavored yogurts found in your grocery store are sweetened with sugar—sometimes a lot of it. You can flavor your own yogurt to suit your taste with your food processor. Sweet fresh fruits don't really need all that sugar. Using the steel blade, simply process rinsed fruits, like raspberries, strawberries, blueberries or peaches, and unflavored or homemade yogurt. Pour into serving size containers and refrigerate.

BABY FOOD

If you have a baby, it is possible to create your own wholesome, pure baby food with your processor that will save you money and provide your baby with a preservative- and additive-free diet.

Simply steam or simmer fresh vegetables in a small amount of stock or water, drain well and purée with steel blade.

Poultry, fish or meat can also be puréed and softened with milk or broth. Fresh or dried fruits can be poached and puréed as well. As you prepare your own meals, set appropriate ingredients aside before seasoning, then purée and store in labeled airtight containers in refrigerator for baby's next dinner, or freeze in individual serving portions in labeled freeze/cook bags for later use.

FRESH COCONUT

If you like packaged coconut, you'll probably *love* fresh coconut. Ever wonder how to deal with a fresh one? Well here's how, and it's easy! All you will need is a screwdriver and a hammer.

1. Tap a hole in each "eye" of the coconut—there are three. Then drain the coconut by turning upside down. This liquid is not coconut milk; however, it can be reserved after being strained and heated in a saucepan over a low flame until reduced to half of original volume. It will have a strong coconut flavor and can be used as a flavoring ingredient.
2. After draining coconut, put it on a cookie sheet and bake in the oven at 350° for 20–30 minutes or until shell cracks.
3. Remove from oven, wrap in a towel and tap with hammer.
4. Pull off outer shell and you will be left with the coconut meat, covered with a skin.
5. Peel off skin with a vegetable peeler. The coconut meat can then be grated by hand or cut into pieces and processed in your food processor with steel blade or shredding disc.

Coconut milk is made by soaking shredded coconut in milk, water or cream overnight. Then strain, pressing as much liquid out as possible. Discard shredded coconut, as it will have lost much of its flavor. What's left is coconut milk! Skip says once you've tasted the difference and compared the cost, you may never buy packaged coconut again!

SHREDDED COCONUT

Using shredding disc, stand pieces of peeled coconut upright in feed tube. Use firm (but not hard) pressure on food pusher. Place in airtight container or bag, label and freeze.

For *grated* coconut, use steel blade. Peel coconut, cut into 1-inch cubes, place in work bowl and process until desired consistency. Freeze same as shredded coconut.

BREAD CRACKER CRUMBS

Using steel blade, place crackers or pieces of stale, toasted bread in work bowl and process to desired texture. For seasoned bread crumbs, chop fresh herbs with crumbs in work bowl. For buttered crumbs, drizzle melted butter through feed tube with machine running.

Store in labeled airtight container in cupboard; also may be frozen.

FRESH HERBS

It's great to have fresh herbs on hand all year round, especially chopped and ready to use. Herbs freeze well, so it's a good idea to buy plenty when they're in season.

Rinse herbs well in cool water and dry carefully. Remove large stems. Place herbs in work bowl and process with steel blade to desired consistency. Remove to airtight container or bag, label and freeze. They can be used frozen in hot dishes or thawed when needed.

I always have at least parsley, basil and dill on hand. Chives are the only herbs I have found difficult to process—because of their shape, they tend to shred rather than chop.

If you have a garden or a sunny window sill, you might explore the possibility of an herb garden. It is really quite easy to cultivate. For me, an herb garden is one of the finest things in life.

COOKING CONDIMENTS

Cooking gets so much easier when a lot of the work is done ahead of time. Having these condiments on hand and ready to use provides the utmost convenience for fast meals.

Garlic. Peel cloves and, using steel blade, drop through feed tube with machine running. Process to desired consistency. Place in a jar, cover with oil and refrigerate.

Onions. Peel onions, cut off root, cut into quarters and, using a steel blade, process only until coarsely chopped. (Over-processing produces mushy onions.) Place in labeled, airtight container or bag. Freeze in small portions for convenient use.

Peppers. Remove stem, slice off top and scoop out seeds and white fiber. Slice into 2-inch pieces, place in work bowl fitted with steel blade, and process to desired consistency. Store in labeled, airtight container or bag and freeze in small portions.

Ginger root. A wonderful condiment now readily available in most parts of the country. Peel root, cut into 1-inch pieces, place in work bowl and process with steel blade until minced. Store in labeled, airtight container or bag and freeze in small portions.

"ICE" CUBES

Having suffered through too many tasteless cocktails made even more bland by melted ice cubes, we turned to the processor to solve the problem!

(Standard 14-cube tray holds 1½ cups liquid.)

Tomato Cubes

---

    1 pound ripe tomatoes (peeled, quartered and seeded), or 1½
      cups tomato juice

1. With steel blade in place, add tomatoes to work bowl. Process until finely chopped but not puréed.
2. Pour into ice cube tray and freeze.
3. When completely frozen, transfer cubes to freezer bag or container. Serve in Bloody Marys or float one cube in each bowl the next time you serve gazpacho.

Fruit Cubes

An excellent use for fruit that's overripe or slightly bruised!

2 medium apples (cored and cubed; peeled if skin is tough)

1 medium ripe banana (peeled and cut in several pieces)
¼ cup freshly squeezed lime juice

1. With steel blade in place, add all ingredients to work bowl. Lock cover in place. Process 30 seconds.
2. Stop processor. Remove cover and scrape down sides of work bowl with spatula. Replace cover and process 1 minute or until mixture is completely smooth.
3. Pour into ice cube tray and freeze. When completely frozen, transfer cubes to freezer bag or container. Serve in Daiquiris, Margaritas, Whiskey Sours, or any other cocktail that might benefit from a tart touch of fruity flavor.

Cucumber Cubes

2 large cucumbers (peeled, seeded   1 stalk celery (string removed and
  and cut into 2-inch chunks)   cut into 2-inch pieces)

1. Process with steel blade until smooth.
2. Freeze as for Tomato Cubes. Use with or instead of Tomato Cubes in mixed drinks or chilled vegetable soups.

Variations (Use your imagination!):

Combine complementary fruits or purée individual ones. Add a little fruit juice or spice.

Peaches, peeled and pitted, with 2 or 3 tablespoons of lemon or lime juice and a dash of cinnamon or fresh mint leaves are especially tasty.

Melons of all kinds, strawberries, raspberries and seedless grapes are also excellent candidates for cubes.

Chapter 3

APPETIZERS

Zucchini Fritters

Ingredients:

1 cup cornflakes or corn chips
1 pound zucchini (trimmed)
¼ cup grated Parmesan
½ bunch parsley (rinsed, dried and stems removed)

1 large clove garlic (peeled)
1 large egg
¼ teaspoon salt
⅛ teaspoon pepper
3 cups oil for deep frying

TAMARI DIPPING SAUCE:

1 large scallion (trimmed and cut into 1-inch pieces)
1 1-inch piece fresh ginger root (peeled)

½ cup tamari
2 tablespoons water

1. Add cornflakes to work bowl fitted with steel blade. Process until finely crumbed. Remove to 1-quart bowl and set aside.
2. Replace steel blade with shredding disc. Cut zucchini to fit vertically in feed tube. Pack feed tube and process with light pressure on food pusher for fine shreds. Repeat until all zucchini is shredded. Remove to bowl with cornflake crumbs. Add Parmesan cheese and stir to combine.
3. Replace shredding disc with steel blade. Add parsley to work bowl. Cover and start processor. Immediately drop garlic down feed tube and process until finely minced.
4. Break egg into work bowl containing parsley and garlic. Add salt and pepper. Process 4–5 seconds until egg is frothy and mixture is well combined. Pour over zucchini and crumb mixture. Mix well. Cover with plastic wrap and refrigerate ½ hour.
5. Meanwhile, prepare sauce. Add scallion to work bowl fitted with steel blade. Cover and start processor. Immediately drop ginger down feed tube and process until finely minced.
6. Scrape down sides of work bowl with spatula. Add tamari and water. Process 3 seconds to combine. Pour into small bowl, cover and refrigerate.
7. Heat oil in wok or deep fryer to 375°. Drop chilled zucchini mixture by the tablespoonful into hot oil—*a few* tablespoons at a time. (Too many at once will lower the temperature of the oil, resulting in soggy fritters.) Fry about 10 seconds or until golden. Remove with slotted spoon. Place on cookie sheet lined with paper towel and keep warm in 200° oven. Repeat until all fritters are done.
8. Serve hot with Tamari Dipping Sauce.

YIELD: *approximately 24 fritters*

Eggplant Caviar

A tasty mock caviar—no fish eggs needed here! It's delicious spread on whole wheat crackers.

Ingredients:

2 large eggplants (rinsed and patted dry)
2 teaspoons oil
½ bunch fresh parsley (rinsed, dried and stems removed)
½ bunch mint (rinsed, dried and stems removed; 1 tablespoon dried can be substituted)
1 onion (peeled and quartered)
3 cloves garlic (peeled)
1½ teaspoons salt
½ teaspoon pepper
¼ cup sesame tahini (sesame paste available at health food stores—can be omitted if unavailable)
¼ teaspoon cinnamon
2 tablespoons vinegar
Juice of 1 lemon
2 teaspoons toasted sesame seeds (see note)
½ cup pumpkin seeds (hulled and toasted; see note)
Whole wheat crackers for serving

1. Preheat oven to 350°.
2. Rub eggplants with oil.
3. Place eggplants in casserole dish and bake 50 minutes or until tender.
4. When done, remove from oven. Let cool.
5. With steel blade, process parsley and mint coarsely.
6. Add onion and garlic and process until finely chopped. Remove to large bowl.
7. Split cooled eggplants and scoop pulp out. Place in processor bowl. Add salt, pepper, tahini, cinnamon, vinegar and lemon juice. Process until smooth.
8. Remove to bowl with onion mixture. Mix together.
9. Stir in sesame seeds and pumpkin seeds.
10. Refrigerate at least 1–2 hours. Serve with whole wheat crackers.

YIELD: *about 3 cups*

NOTE: Both pumpkin and sesame seeds can be toasted on a cookie sheet in your oven until golden, or in a frying pan with *no* oil, stirred frequently until golden brown.

Eileen Friedman's Baked
Sesame Cheese Ball Appetizers

Every teacher has a favorite student and mine is Eileen Friedman. Eileen swore that she was absolutely incapable in the kitchen, but was willing to try.

Try she did and she has become an accomplished chef, treating her friends and family to gourmet home cooking quite often these days!

She likes this recipe because it's healthy and beautiful and lots of fun to enjoy at a party. I like her for the very same reasons.

Ingredients:

½ bunch fresh parsley (rinsed, dried, and stems removed)
½ pound sharp Cheddar cheese (purchased in 1 piece and cut into cubes)
½ teaspoon Worcestershire sauce
1 tablespoon Dijon mustard
½ cup butter (in pieces)
1 cup unbleached white flour
⅛ teaspoon pepper
¼ cup toasted sesame seeds

1. With steel blade in place, add parsley and cheese cubes to work bowl and process until well grated. Stop machine.
2. Add Worcestershire sauce, mustard, flour, butter pieces and pepper to work bowl. Process until all is combined. Stop machine.
3. Refrigerate mixture for several hours or until firm.
4. Shape with hands into ½-inch balls. Roll in sesame seeds. Refrigerate until ready to use.
5. Bake on cookie sheet at 350° for 10 minutes.
6. Serve warm.

YIELD: *24–30 appetizers*

Olive Anchovy Canapés

Ingredients:

2 2-ounce cans flat anchovy fillets
6 ripe black olives (pitted and mashed)
2 medium cloves garlic (peeled)
1 scallion (finely minced)
1 tablespoon tomato paste
2 tablespoons Parmesan cheese (grated)

1½ tablespoons olive oil
2 teaspoons lemon juice
¼ teaspoon pepper
6 slices whole wheat bread (cut into triangles)
2 tablespoons fresh chopped parsley for garnish

1. Drain oil from anchovies and soak for 5 minutes in cold water. Drain well.
2. Place anchovies, olives, garlic, scallions, tomato paste and cheese in food processor with steel blade in place and process.
3. Add oil slowly through feed tube (as in making mayonnaise).
4. Add lemon juice and pepper. Mix well.
5. Toast bread in oven on one side.
6. Remove and preheat oven to 450°. Spread untoasted side of bread slices with anchovy mixture. Place on ungreased cookie sheet.
7. Bake in 450° oven for 10–12 minutes.
8. Garnish with parsley.

YIELD: *24 canapés*

Crab Stuffed Mushrooms

Ingredients:

20 mushrooms
½ bunch fresh dill (rinsed, dried and stems removed)
½ bunch fresh parsley (rinsed, dried and stems removed)
1 clove garlic (peeled)
½ pound fresh or frozen cooked crabmeat (if frozen, rinse under cold water)
¾ cup mayonnaise
½ cup grated Parmesan cheese
Freshly ground pepper and salt to taste
2 teaspoons Dijon mustard
1 tablespoon Worcestershire sauce
½ teaspoon celery seed

Preheat oven to broil.

1. Wipe mushrooms clean. Remove stems and reserve. Reserve caps for stuffing with crabmeat mixture.
2. With steel blade in place, add mushroom stems, dill and parsley to work bowl. Process, and with motor running, drop in garlic through feed tube. Process until minced.
3. Add rest of ingredients (except caps) to work bowl and process just until combined.
4. Stuff mushroom caps with crabmeat mixture.
5. Place on lightly greased broiling tray.
6. Broil in oven until lightly browned, about 3–5 minutes.

YIELD: *20 appetizers*

Avocado and Tofu Dipping Sauce from "EATS!"

"EATS!" is Skip's very own New York catering company. It is a pleasure to have several of his party recipes included here.

Ingredients:

3 large scallions (whites and greens trimmed and cut into 1-inch pieces)

2–3 hot green chilies or jalapenos (stems and seeds removed, cut into 1-inch pieces) (see note)

1 2-inch piece fresh ginger root (peeled and coarsely chopped) Zest from 1 lemon (cut into strips)

1 3½-ounce can smoked baby clams or oysters (drained)

½ cup cilantro leaves (also known as fresh coriander or chinese parsley)

½ cup parsley leaves

8 ounces tofu (well drained and squeezed)

3 large ripe avocados (peeled and pitted—reserve 1 pit—and cut into 2-inch pieces)

½ cup freshly squeezed lemon juice

1 teaspoon salt

1. With steel blade in place, add scallions, chilies, ginger root, lemon zest, baby clams, cilantro and parsley to work bowl. Lock cover in place and process for 5 1-second bursts. Remove cover and check consistency. Mixture should be uniformly finely minced. If necessary, scrape down sides of work bowl, replace cover and process several more bursts until proper consistency is achieved.
2. Remove work bowl from base, remove steel blade and scrape minced mixture into small bowl. Set aside.
3. Return work bowl to base, insert steel blade and crumble tofu into work bowl. Lock cover in place and process 30 seconds to 1 minute or until completely smooth and fluffy.
4. Remove work bowl from base, remove steel blade and scrape tofu into 3-quart bowl. Set aside.
5. Return work bowl to base and insert steel blade. Add avocado pieces and lemon juice to work bowl. (If your processor has a large-capacity work bowl you should be able to process in 2 batches, adding half the lemon juice to each batch.) Lock cover in place and process 30 seconds to 1 minute or until completely smooth. Remove work bowl from base, remove steel blade and scrape puréed avocado into bowl with tofu.
6. Add finely minced scallion mixture and salt to avocado-tofu purée. Combine well. Bury reserved avocado pit in mixture (helps prevent darkening). Cover and chill several hours or, better yet, overnight in refrigerator.
7. Serve as dipping sauce for crudités, cheese cubes, pita triangles or taco chips.

YIELD: *about 3 cups*

NOTE: Four chili peppers will make the sauce medium hot. Add more or less to your taste. Remember to rinse hands well with cold water, then wash them with soap and hot water after seeding and chopping chilies. Should you touch your face or rub your eyes with chili juices still on your fingers, you will learn the unpleasant way that chilies inflame more than taste buds.

Hidden Garden Pâté from "EATS!"

Ingredients:

¼ pound chicken livers
¼ cup Madeira wine
¾ pound pork fat (partially frozen)
½ pound boneless coarsely ground pork shoulder (see *Grind Your Own Meats and Poultry* . . . , page 95)
½ pound boneless coarsely ground veal shoulder
2 large cloves garlic (peeled)
¼ cup heavy cream
2 large eggs
3 tablespoons flour

1 tablespoon freshly ground pepper
2 teaspoons salt
1 teaspoon dried thyme leaves
½ teaspoon allspice
½ pound smoked tongue (trimmed, cut in 1-inch cubes and well chilled)
½ pound boneless, skinless chicken breast (partially frozen)
1 pound nitrite-free bacon (thinly sliced)

HIDDEN GARDEN STUFFING:

1 10-ounce package frozen spinach (thawed, drained and squeezed)
1 cup fresh basil leaves (rinsed and dried)
½ bunch parsley (rinsed, dried and stems removed)

1 large scallion (trimmed and cut in 1-inch pieces)
2 tablespoons fresh mint (or 2 teaspoons dried)
½ teaspoon salt
¼ cup heavy cream

1. Marinate the chicken livers and garlic in Madeira for 45 minutes while you proceed with the Hidden Garden Stuffing.
2. With the steel blade in place, add the spinach, basil, parsley, scallion, mint and salt to work bowl. Cover and start processor. Pour heavy cream down feed tube and process until mixture is puréed. Remove to small bowl, cover and refrigerate.
3. Cut off a ¼-pound piece from the pork fat and dice it into ¼-inch cubes. Set aside.
4. Cut the remaining pork fat in 1-inch cubes. Grind with the veal and pork according to directions on page 95. Remove ground meat to large bowl and set aside.
5. With steel blade in place, add chicken livers, Madeira, garlic, heavy cream, eggs, flour, pepper, salt, thyme and allspice to work bowl. Process until livers are puréed and mixture is completely smooth. Pour over ground meat in large bowl.
6. With steel blade in place, add smoked tongue to work bowl. Process for 5–6 on/off bursts until very coarsely chopped. Pieces should be about the same size as the diced pork fat. Add the tongue, along with the diced pork fat, to the ground meat mixture in the large bowl. Combine mixture well.
7. Switch to the slicing disc. Load feed tube with partially frozen chicken and process with medium pressure on food pusher. Remove chicken slices and set aside.

To Assemble Pâté:

8. Preheat oven to 350°. Line the bottom and sides of a 6-cup loaf pan with slightly overlapping slices of nitrite-free bacon. Allow slices to overhang lip of loaf pan.

9. Spoon half of ground meat mixture into loaf pan. Cover with half of chicken slices. Remove Hidden Garden Stuffing from refrigerator. Spoon it lengthwise down center of loaf pan to within ½-inch of the bacon lining. Cover stuffing with remaining chicken slices. Fill loaf pan with remaining ground meat mixture, mounding it like the top of a loaf of bread. Fold the overhanging bacon slices up over the pâté mixture. Cover any bare spots with some of the remaining bacon slices.

10. Tightly cover the loaf pan with 2 layers of aluminum foil. Place loaf pan in large, deep roasting pan. Fill roasting pan with boiling water to reach halfway up the loaf pan. Bake at 350° for 1½ hours.

11. Pâté is done if juices run clear when you press down on foil covering. If juices are still pink, return pâté to oven and bake 15 minutes longer. When pâté is done, remove from oven, drain water from roasting pan. Set pâté back in roasting pan and let cool 15 minutes. Place a 2-pound weight on top of pâté. (I use a brick wrapped in foil. If you don't have access to a brick, set a cutting board over the pâté and set a quart jar filled with water on top, as it weighs approximately 2 pounds.) Cool for 1 hour, then refrigerate—weighted—overnight.

12. To unmold, remove weights and aluminum foil. Set loaf pan in hot water for several minutes. Remove and invert over large platter. Shake until pâté loosens. Remove loaf pan. Wipe excess fat and gelled juices from pâté. Slice very thin. Serve on lettuce or with black bread, thinly sliced sweet onion and cornichons.

YIELD: *1 9 x 5 x 3-inch pâté*

Skip's Clam Soufflés

Ingredients:

3 dozen clams
1 cup dry white wine
4 scallions (trimmed and cut into 1-inch pieces)
1 bunch parsley (stems removed)
½ bunch dill (stems removed)
1 tablespoon Dijon mustard
1 teaspoon freshly ground pepper
3 large eggs (separated)
¼ teaspoon salt

1. Preheat oven to 375°. Steam clams in wine until open. Drain. Remove 18 clams from shells and place in work bowl fitted with steel blade. Leave 18 clams in half shells and arrange on cookie sheet.
2. Add scallions, parsley and dill to clams in work bowl. Cover and process for 5 1-second bursts. Remove cover, scrape down sides of work bowl with spatula. Replace cover and process for several more seconds until mixture is finely chopped.
3. Scrape mixture into 3 quart bowl. Add mustard and pepper. Mix well.
4. Separate eggs. Beat egg yolks into clam mixture and place whites in a 2-quart bowl.
5. Beat whites with salt until they hold stiff peaks and fold into clam mixture.
6. Fill each of the reserved clam shells with about 2 tablespoons of the mixture, covering completely the whole clam.
7. Bake in 375° oven 10 minutes, or until soufflés are puffed and just beginning to brown. Serve immediately.

YIELD: *18 soufflés on the half shell*

Steak Tartare

Ingredients:

6 shallots (peeled)
1 small fennel bulb (trimmed and quartered)
½ bunch parsley (rinsed, dried and stems removed)
½ cup celery leaves
3 egg yolks
3 tablespoons Dijon-style mustard

3 tablespoons lemon juice
3 tablespoons capers (drained)
1 tablespoon freshly ground pepper
1 teaspoon salt
¼ cup olive oil
1½ pound top round or sirloin tip roast (cut into 1-inch cubes and well chilled)

FOR SERVING:
toasted black bread triangles
cucumber slices (¼-inch thick)

GARNISH FOR CANAPES:
black radish slices (¼-inch thick)
additional whole capers and a few
sprigs parsley

1. With steel blade in place, add shallots, fennel, parsley and celery leaves to work bowl. Process with on/off bursts until finely minced. Remove to 2-quart bowl and set aside.
2. With steel blade in place, add egg yolks, mustard, lemon juice, capers, pepper and salt to work bowl. Process 10 seconds. Stop machine and scrape down sides of work bowl.
3. Cover and start processor. Slowly pour oil down feed tube. Process until all oil is added and mixture is emulsified. Pour into small bowl and set aside.
4. With steel blade in place, add beef cubes to work bowl. Process in batches until all beef is coarsely ground. Remove to 2-quart bowl with minced herbs.
5. Pour egg yolk mixture over ground beef and herbs. Combine well.
6. Mound tartare in center of platter and surround with black bread triangles, sliced cucumber and radishes. Let guests help themselves.

or

7. Top each triangle and vegetable slice with 1 tablespoon Tartare and garnish with a sprig of parsley or several whole capers. Serve as canapés.

YIELD: *36 appetizers or 6 first courses*

Homemade Hummous with Pita

Ingredients:

2 cups drained chickpeas (cooked fresh or canned)
½ teaspoon salt
⅛ teaspoon pepper
3 tablespoons tahini
¼ cup lemon juice

3 cloves garlic (peeled)
2 tablespoons cold water
2 tablespoons olive oil
6 whole wheat pitas (cut into triangles)

GARNISH:
fresh parsley (rinsed, dried and stems removed)

1. With steel blade in place, add chickpeas, salt, pepper, tahini and lemon juice to work bowl. Process and with motor running, drop in garlic.
2. Then pour water and oil in through feed tube with motor running. Process until smooth.
3. Pour into serving bowl.
4. With steel blade in place, add parsley to clean work bowl and process until coarsely chopped.
5. Heat pita triangles by placing on baking sheet and putting into 350° oven for 3–5 minutes.
6. Garnish serving bowl with parsley in center. Serve with lightly heated pita triangles.

YIELD: *24 appetizers*

My Momma's Stuffed Mushrooms

Throughout my childhood, holidays were celebrated with beautiful feasts. They started with my father's special Italian antipasto and continued with stuffed mushrooms, fresh vegetables, sweet potatoes and a huge turkey stuffed only as my mother can do (Momma's Perfect Turkey Stuffing is included on page 131). To this day, my mother considers herself a simple cook.

During the writing of each new cookbook, I make a special trip home to pry my mother's "simple" recipes out of her. In reality they *are* simple to prepare, but my mother's intuitive knowledge of how to prepare fresh foods to perfection makes them very special. I hope you enjoy these stuffed mushrooms as much as I always do.

Ingredients:

1 small bunch fresh parsley (rinsed, dried and stems removed)

1 pound medium or large fresh mushrooms (brushed clean, stems removed and set aside)

½ cup Italian bread crumbs

⅛ teaspoon salt

⅛ teaspoon pepper

1 tablespoon grated Parmesan cheese

1–2 tablespoons oil

3 tablespoons water

1. With steel blade in place, add parsley to work bowl and process until coarsely chopped. Stop machine.
2. Add mushroom stems, bread crumbs, salt, pepper and cheese to work bowl. Process to combine.
3. Place mushroom caps in baking pan face up. Place mixture in each one and top each with a drizzle of oil.
4. Add water to baking pan and bake 20 minutes at 350°. Serve.

YIELD: *20–24 mushrooms*

Clams Casino Viscardi

Here Papa Viscardi steps into the limelight with another family favorite! Having grown up in the Chesapeake Bay area, we enjoyed it often.

Ingredients:

1 dozen clams scrubbed
1 small onion (peeled and quartered)
1 small bunch parsley (rinsed, dried and stems removed; reserve half bunch for garnish)

1 clove garlic (peeled)
½ cup Italian bread crumbs
¼ teaspoon oregano
¼ cup grated Parmesan cheese
2 tablespoons olive oil

GARNISH:

1 lemon (quartered)
reserved half-bunch parsley

1. Steam clams in pot until they open. Remove clams. Reserve 12 half shells.
2. With steel blade in place, add onion and ½ bunch parsley to work bowl and process, adding garlic through feed tube with motor running. Stop machine when all is minced.
3. Add bread crumbs, clams, oregano, cheese and oil to work bowl. Process until combined.
4. Spoon mixture into each clam shell.
5. Place shells on broiling pan and broil 5 minutes or until golden.
6. Garnish serving tray with quartered lemon and parsley.

YIELD: *12 appetizers*

Chapter 4

BREAKFAST

Eggs Alaska

One of the most prized discoveries Skip and I ever made was that beaten egg whites create perfect "nests" for egg yolks for an innovative and slenderizing variation on Eggs Benedict. In this, the split muffins are topped with spinach, ham or vegetables, topped with fluffy mounds of seasoned egg whites that are indented in the center to create nests for the yolks and then baked. It's spectacular!

Ingredients:

1 large onion (peeled and quartered)
1 dozen mushrooms
4 ounces Cheddar cheese
Oil for cooking
½ teaspoon salt

Pepper to taste
½ teaspoon basil
2 whole wheat English muffins
Butter for toasted muffins
4 eggs (separated carefully—each yolk should be set aside singly)

1. Preheat oven to 450°. With slicing disc in place, pack feed tube with onion and process until sliced.
2. Leaving onions in work bowl, process mushrooms the same way. Remove to bowl and set aside.
3. Switch to shredding disc and shred cheddar cheese. Set aside.
4. Saute onions and mushrooms until golden. Season with ¼ teaspoon salt, pepper to taste and basil, and set aside.
5. Toast muffins lightly and butter.
6. With electric beater, beat egg whites until fluffy. Add remaining salt and beat until they hold stiff peaks. Fold in shredded cheese.
7. To assemble: Divide vegetable mixture among muffin halves. Pile egg white mixture on each. Make an indentation in whites to serve as a nest for a yolk. Place a yolk in each nest.
8. Bake 7–10 minutes or until yolk is set.

YIELD: *2–4 servings*

Skip's Tricolor Eggs Olympus

Ingredients:

2 whole wheat English muffins
2 tablespoons butter
6 ounces sharp Cheddar cheese
3 carrots (scrubbed and cut into 2-inch lengths)
1 bunch watercress (rinsed, dried and stems removed)
1 bunch parsley (rinsed, dried and stems removed)

2 scallions (ends removed and cut into 2-inch lengths)
4 eggs separated (yolks reserved and separated as well)
½ teaspoon marjoram leaves (crushed)
½ teaspoon pepper
Salt to taste

1. Split and toast muffins lightly. Butter and set aside.
2. With shredding disc in place, pack feed tube with cheese and process until all is shredded. Remove from work bowl and set aside.
3. Switch to steel blade. Add carrots to work bowl. Process until finely chopped. Remove from work bowl and combine with half of the shredded cheese and set aside.
4. Add watercress, parsley and scallions to work bowl and process until puréed.
5. With electric mixer, beat egg whites until frothy. Add a little salt and beat until stiff peaks form. Sprinkle with marjoram, ¼ teaspoon pepper and the remaining shredded cheese. Fold in gently but quickly until well combined.
6. Cover each muffin half with ¼ of the carrot mixture.
7. Top each with ¼ of the watercress mixture.
8. Spoon ¼ of the whites onto each half making a small indentation in each to hold yolk.
9. Slip a yolk into each of the nests. Sprinkle with the remaining ¼ teaspoon pepper and salt to taste.
10. Bake at 350° for 12–15 minutes or until yolks are set to desired consistency. Serve.

YIELD: *2 servings*

Baked Eggs with Avocado and Cheese

Manhattan's Fifth Avenue is known all over the country for its fabulous shops where one can find the best of everything. The lower part of Fifth Avenue is perhaps less known but equally interesting, as it is filled with photographers' studios that capture the best on film to produce magazine layouts and book covers that circulate worldwide. One of the photographers that section houses is my friend, Gary Abatelli. His specialty is "still life," and if I can cook it, he can capture it—perfectly!

One of Gary's accounts is Maxwell House, and in honor of a job well done, I created Baked Eggs with Avocado and Cheese to go with that great coffee. When you try it, you will be amazed at how great it is, and how very easy!

Ingredients:

½ bunch parsley (rinsed, dried and stems removed)
1 4-ounce piece Cheddar cheese
1 ripe avocado (peeled, pitted and sliced thinly)

4 eggs
⅔ cup half and half cream
Salt to taste
Dash of pepper

1. With steel blade in place, add parsley to work bowl and process until coarsely chopped. Stop machine, remove and set aside.
2. Change to shredding disc, add cheese through feed tube, processing until all shredded. Stop machine.
3. Place half the shredded cheese in buttered 8 x 8 x 2-inch casserole dish and top with avocado slices.
4. Slip in eggs with yolks unbroken.
5. Pour cream over slowly and sprinkle with salt and pepper.
6. Top with remaining cheese, sprinkling evenly all over.
7. Sprinkle with parsley.
8. Bake in oven at 350° for 10 minutes, then place under broiler for quick browning for 1 minute.
9. Cut in half. Lift out with spatula and serve.

YIELD: *2 servings*

The Eggy Eggplant Casserole

This next one takes a little time because the eggplants need to bake 45 minutes and then cool. You can, however, bake the eggplants the night before, scoop out the pulp and refrigerate until needed. If you are serving it as a brunch entrée, you can simply bake the eggplants earlier that morning. It's worth the extra planning because it really is delectable!

Ingredients:

2 medium eggplants (about 1½ pounds)
2 ounces sharp Cheddar cheese
2 teaspoons salt
1 teaspoon pepper
3 tablespoons lemon juice
4 eggs (separated)

1 tablespoon sesame seeds
½ bunch parsley (rinsed, dried and stems removed)
2 cloves garlic (peeled)
2 tablespoons butter for buttering casserole

1. Rinse eggplants, pat dry and place on baking tray in preheated 350° oven. Bake 45 minutes or until tender.
2. Meanwhile, with shredding disc in place, pack feed tube with cheese and process. Remove from work bowl. Set aside.
3. Switch to steel blade. When eggplant is ready, split, scoop out pulp and add to work bowl. Allow pulp to cool.
4. Add salt, pepper, lemon juice, egg yolks, sesame seeds and parsley. Process, and with motor running, add garlic by dropping through feed tube. Process until smooth.
5. Add shredded cheese and process briefly just to combine. Remove mixture to 2-quart bowl.
6. Beat egg whites until they hold soft peaks and fold into mixture.
7. Pour into buttered casserole and bake in 350° oven for 45 minutes. Serve immediately.

YIELD: *2–4 servings*

Spanish Eggs

Ingredients:

1 onion (peeled and quartered)
1 green pepper (cored, quartered, seeds removed and cut into 2-inch pieces)
4 tablespoons butter
4 eggs

1 tomato (cored and quartered)
¼ cup whole wheat bread crumbs
¼ teaspoon oregano
½ teaspoon basil
Salt and pepper to taste
½ cup grated Parmesan cheese

1. With steel blade in place add onion and pepper to work bowl. Process until coarsely chopped.
2. Sauté onion and pepper mixture in butter in frying pan or wok until tender.
3. Spread the mixture over bottom of casserole dish.
4. Break eggs over mixture, being careful not to break yolks.
5. With steel blade in place, add tomato. Process 2–3 1-second bursts to chop coarsely. Add bread crumbs, oregano, basil, salt and pepper to taste and Parmesan. Process 2–3 1-second bursts just to combine.
6. Sprinkle over eggs.
7. Bake in preheated 375° oven for 10 minutes or until crumbs are golden, cheese is melted and eggs are set.

YIELD: *2 servings*

Baked Ham and Eggs

Ingredients:

1 onion (peeled and quartered)
½ bunch parsley (rinsed, dried & stems removed)
½ cup ham pieces
2 ounces Cheddar cheese

4 tablespoons butter
4 eggs
Salt and cayenne pepper to taste
½ cup heavy cream

1. With steel blade in place, add onion, parsley and ham to work bowl. Process in short bursts until coarsely chopped. Stop machine and remove to bowl. Set aside.
2. Switch to shredding disc, pack feed tube with cheese and process.
3. Heat butter in frying pan or wok and sauté onion and ham mixture until onion is tender.
4. Pour into casserole dish and top with half the cheese.
5. Break eggs over cheese, being careful not to break yolks. Sprinkle with salt and pepper.
6. Pour heavy cream over and top with rest of cheese.
7. Bake in preheated 375° oven for 10 minutes or until eggs are set to desired consistency. Serve by cutting in half and lifting out with spatula.

YIELD: *serves 2*

Cristina's Guacamole Omelette

Ingredients:

½ small onion
1 medium tomato
2 ounces jack cheese
1 large ripe avocado
¼ cup sour cream
1½ tablespoons green chili sauce
(see note)

1 teaspoon lemon juice
Dash salt
3 tablespoons butter
6 eggs (lightly beaten)
1 tablespoon water
Dash Tabasco sauce

1. With steel blade in place, coarsely chop onion by pulsing on/off 3–4 times. Set aside.
2. Remove onion from work bowl. Add tomato and process for 3–4 on/off bursts to chop coarsely. Remove from bowl and set aside.
3. With shredding disc in place shred cheese. Set aside.
4. Switch to steel blade. Cut avocado in half. Remove pit and scoop out pulp using spoon. Place in bowl of processor.
5. Add sour cream, green chili sauce, lemon juice and salt to bowl. Process 5 seconds or until smooth. Turn into small bowl.
6. In small skillet sauté onion in 1 tablespoon butter until transparent. Add tomato and sauté another minute or so until heated through.
7. Fold tomato and onion mixture into avocado mixture.
8. Beat eggs well with water and Tabasco.
9. Melt remaining butter in omelette pan. Pour in eggs and cook until set. Spoon in guacamole filling, reserving 2 tablespoons for topping. Sprinkle cheese over guacamole, reserving 2 tablespoons for garnish.
10. Fold omelette and turn onto serving plate.
11. With knife, thinly spread reserved guacamole on top of omelette, sprinkle with reserved cheese. Divide in half.
12. Serve immediately.

YIELD: *2 large omelettes*

NOTE: Sauce can be purchased in most markets. It is a red-colored salsa, but is made with green chiles and is medium to mild in taste.

Strawberry Pancakes with Fresh Berry Sauce

This is a healthy, bountiful breakfast. Be sure to make the Berry Sauce first so it'll be ready to top hotcakes!

Ingredients:

2 eggs
1 tablespoon oil
1 cup milk
1½ cups unbleached white flour
⅛ teaspoon salt
1 teaspoon baking powder

1 teaspoon vanilla
½ pint strawberries (rinsed, hulled and halved)
1 tablespoon honey
Oil for cooking

1. With plastic blade in place (you can use steel blade if you don't have a plastic blade), add eggs, oil and milk to work bowl. Process just until blended.
2. Stop machine. Add flour, salt, baking powder and vanilla. Process until blended.
3. Add halved strawberries and honey. Process about 5 seconds—little berry chunks should be left in batter.
4. Preheat oven to 200°. Heat 1 tablespoon oil in cast iron skillet or pancake griddle. Pour batter to form pancakes. Flip when batter begins bubbling around edges. Place in warm oven to keep hot.
5. Serve with Berry Sauce and sour cream (see following recipe).

YIELD: *12 pancakes*

Berry Sauce

Ingredients:

½ pint strawberries
½ cup honey

⅓ cup water
½ cup sour cream

1. With steel blade in place, add strawberries to work bowl and process in 4 1-second bursts or until coarsely chopped.
2. In small saucepan, place honey and water and bring to boil over medium heat. Boil 5 minutes.
3. Add to strawberries. Process just for an instant. Pour over hot pancakes with a dollop of sour cream.

YIELD: *sauce for 12 pancakes*

Chapter 5

LUNCH

Ever wonder what to put in your kid's lunches?

We experimented with the grinding of many kinds of nuts and found several wonderful combinations. Served on whole grain bread, they're high protein boosts that delight children from eight to eighty!

NUT BUTTERS

A general hint when making nut butters: Toast nuts or seeds in a 350° oven for 7–10 minutes before processing. The toasting brings out the flavor.

Following are some of our favorites—simple nut butters or combinations of nuts, seeds or spices. They keep well, tightly covered, in the refrigerator.

Toasted Almond Butter

Ingredients:

2 cups toasted *unblanched* almonds

Process with steel blade until smooth and creamy.

YIELD: *1 cup*

Add 1 or 2 tablespoons of Toasted Almond Butter to the Simple Garlic Vinaigrette on page 29 for a unique salad dressing. It is also used in one of our favorite sauces (see Cold Noodles Szechuan Style, page 118).

Spanish Peanut-Sesame Butter

Ingredients:

2 cups toasted spanish peanuts *with* skins

½ cup toasted sesame seeds
2 tablespoons tamari

Combine all ingredients in work bowl fitted with steel blade. Process until smooth. Makes a great sandwich with sliced bananas.

YIELD: *about 1 cup*

Pecan Cinnamon Orange Butter

Ingredients:

Zest from 1 orange (cut in strips)
1 teaspoon cinnamon

2 tablespoons granulated sugar
2 cups toasted pecans

With steel blade in place, add orange zest, cinnamon and sugar to work bowl. Process until finely minced. Add pecans and process until smooth. A great eye-opener spread on your morning toast.

YIELD: *1 cup*

Cristina's Cheddar Cheese Sandwich Spread

My friend and food collaborator, Cristina Eisenberg, made this recipe up when she was 12 years old and had to make her brother's lunches every night! She got so sick and tired of boring tuna salad and salami sandwiches that she started experimenting. It is still one of her favorite sandwich spreads and now it's one of my favorites, too.

Ingredients:

1½ pounds mild Cheddar cheese   3 tablespoons sweet pickle relish
 2 hard boiled eggs   1 4-ounce jar chopped pimentos
⅔ cup mayonnaise

1. With shredding disc in place, grate cheese and set aside.
2. With steel blade in place, chop eggs by processing for 3–4 1-second bursts.
3. Add all other ingredients and process approximately 6–8 seconds, until well blended.

YIELD: *enough for 6 sandwiches*

TOFU

Tofu, also called bean curd, is one of the most amazing products one could ever hope to discover. High in protein, low in calories and cholesterol, I consider it "future food." Its popularity is already gaining in leaps and bounds as people discover its versatility. Tofu is made from soybeans and in its natural state has very little flavor. However, it *absorbs* flavors beautifully, therefore, with creative preparation it can taste like anything. It can be marinated and broiled like a steak, mixed into a salad, substituted as a tunafish-like sandwich filling, scrambled like eggs, puréed into sauce for a high protein boost or even sweetened and made into a mock cheesecake that tastes great and spares you the calories. See recipe for Tofu "Mayonnaise" and Variations, page 27, for more tofu ideas.

Tofu is available in grocery stores these days, usually found in the dairy case packaged in a plastic carton in water. It's also found in Chinese, Japanese and Korean vegetable stands and all natural food stores. You will see it in either flat or very thick cakes, Chinese being the first variety, Japanese the second. The taste and methods of preparation are the same for both.

Tofu should be refrigerated in water and will stay for a week if you change the water daily. It can also be frozen in its original container. Thaw completely before using, drain, rinse and squeeze dry.

I know it's hard to be a beginner, but the beginner stage passes fast with tofu and before you know it, you'll be telling everyone you know about this incredible discovery for the nutrition-oriented, calorie-conscious consumer.

Camel Tofu Treats

There is a moving company in New York City called "Camel" and the logo on the truck is "men who enjoy their work." Well, it's true, because the men are a group of friends that has worked together for years. Their clients are New York's best who want to be absolutely secure in the knowledge that everything will get from one place to another—perfectly. Crockett—the owner—guarantees it. His wife Karen and I decided to create the perfect lunch for "men who enjoy their work" and we came up with this next one. It's light, but filling, and sure to satisfy the taste buds. If you've got someone special to pack a lunch for, this is something different that's sure to get rave reviews!

Ingredients:

3 carrots (scrubbed and cut into 2-inch lengths)
1 pound tofu
2 scallions (ends removed and cut into 2-inch lengths)
¼ cup tamari (soy sauce)
¼ teaspoon pepper
2 cloves garlic (peeled)
1 tablespoon Dijon mustard (or 1 tablespoon sesame tahini)
1 cup bean sprouts (see note)

1. With shredding disc in place, pack feed tube with carrots and process. Remove from work bowl and set aside.
2. Switch to steel blade. Add tofu, scallions, tamari, pepper and Dijon mustard (or tahini). Process, and with motor running, drop garlic through feed tube. Process until well combined but not totally smooth. Remove to bowl and stir in one-half the carrots.
3. Serve on whole wheat bread topped with remaining carrots and sprouts, or stuff into whole wheat pita pocket.

YIELD: *4 sandwiches*

NOTE: Available in most grocery stores in the produce department.

Miso Soup

Miso has to be one of the most incredible foods ever created by man. Miso has a unique flavor that makes a great base for soups and also provides a healthful balance of essential oils, minerals, natural sugars, proteins and vitamins.

Miso is a dark brown paste that is usually sold in plastic packets in natural food stores. It's very different and worth searching out. It's actually made from the milk of soy beans.

One tip on Miso Soup-making—never let it boil once you add the miso paste. Boiling destroys some of its most valuable nutritional ingredients, the amino acids and enzymes.

Ingredients:

2 carrots (scrubbed and cut into lengths to fit your feed tube)
1 onion (peeled)
¼ head of cabbage

Peanut oil for cooking
5 cups water
4 tablespoons miso paste

1. With slicing disc in place, pack feed tube with carrots and process.
2. Process onion and cabbage the same way. Remove from work bowl.
3. Heat 2 tablespoons oil in large frying pan or wok. Add vegetables and stir fry 5 minutes.
4. Transfer to soup pot and add ½ cup water. Bring vegetables to boil, lower flame, cover and simmer 15 minutes.
5. Add remaining water and simmer 15 minutes.
6. Remove 1 ladle of stock, place in small bowl. Add miso paste to it. Stir until dissolved.
7. Add to soup, stir, cover and turn off heat.
8. Let sit for 5 minutes, then serve.

YIELD: *at least 6 servings*

NOTE: For variety, different vegetables can be substituted or added and serving bowls can be garnished with chopped scallions.

Cristina's Split Pea Soup

Ingredients:

2½ cups split peas
4 cups water
2 14½-ounce cans vegetable broth
1 teaspoon salt
½ teaspoon freshly ground pepper
1 teaspoon Worcestershire sauce
1 bay leaf

3 carrots (peeled and cut in 1-inch pieces)
4 stalks celery (cut in 1-inch pieces)
1 medium spanish onion (peeled and quartered)
2 slices nitrite-free bacon (cooked, drained and crumbled)
Croutons for garnish

1. Soak peas in 4 cups water for 1–2 hours.
2. Place peas, water and vegetable broth in a large soup pot. Add salt, pepper, Worcestershire sauce, bay leaf and enough extra water to make 8 cups of liquid.
3. Simmer soup over very low heat for 1 hour. Stir frequently to prevent sticking.
4. With steel blade in place, add carrots, celery and onion to work bowl. Process 5–6 1-second bursts or until coarsely chopped.
5. Add chopped carrots, celery, onion and crumbled bacon to soup and simmer for another 1½ hours. Taste and correct seasoning if necessary.
6. With steel blade in place, add 2 cups of the soup to work bowl. Cover and process until smooth. Repeat until all soup is puréed.
7. Return puréed soup to soup pot and heat through.
8. Ladle into warm soup bowls and garnish with croutons.

YIELD: *6 servings*

Grandma's Lentil Soup

Lentil Soup is one soup that doesn't have to simmer all day to be good. In an hour you can sit down to steaming bowls of this high protein delight. Grandma made it at least once a week—she said it would keep us healthy and I believe it did!

Ingredients:

1 cup lentils
6 cups stock or water
1 teaspoon salt
1 stalk celery (cut into lengths to fit your feed tube)

3 small to medium carrots (scrubbed and cut into lengths to fit your feed tube)
2 onions (peeled)
2 tablespoons oil

1. Rinse lentils with cold water.
2. Place 6 cups stock or water, lentils, and salt in soup pot and heat.
3. Bring just to boiling; lower heat, cover and simmer ½ hour.
4. Meanwhile, with slicing disc in place, pack feed tube with celery and process.
5. Process carrots and onions the same way. Remove from work bowl.
6. Heat 2 tablespoons oil in wok or frying pan. Add carrots, celery and onion slices. Sauté 5 minutes.
7. Add to soup pot, simmer 15 more minutes and serve. Or, purée in batches and serve.

YIELD: *4–6 bowls*

Annie Fox's "Crème" of Carrot Soup

No cream in this one but it sure tastes like it! The lovely texture is achieved with rolled oats.

Ingredients:

1 onion (peeled)
Oil for cooking
3 cups raw carrots (cut into chunks)

7 cups water
2 handfuls rolled oats
Dash of salt

GARNISH:
fresh parsley (rinsed, dried and stems removed)

1. With slicing disc in place, pack feed tube with onion and process until sliced.
2. Sauté the onion slices in a little bit of oil in a soup pot.
3. When it softens, add remaining ingredients.
4. Bring to boil. Cover. Reduce heat and simmer 35 minutes or until carrots are tender. Allow to cool.
5. Then, with steel blade in place, add to work bowl in one or two batches. Process until puréed. Reheat to serving temperature.
6. Meanwhile, with steel blade in place, add parsley to clean work bowl and process until coarsely chopped. Use as garnish in center of each serving bowl.

YIELD: *a potful!*

Tabouli Salad

This is a great lunch, especially in summer. Bulgur adds fiber to your diet, which keeps the system clean and healthy. Wonderful for dieters, too.

Ingredients:

3 cups boiling water
1½ cups bulgur wheat
1 bunch fresh dill (rinsed, dried and stems removed)
1 bunch fresh parsley (rinsed, dried and stems removed)
1 cucumber (peeled if waxed)
1 bunch scallions (ends trimmed and cut into lengths to fit feed tube)
2 tablespoons toasted sesame seeds
8–10 cherry tomatoes (halved)
Juice of 2 lemons
¼ cup tamari, or to taste
⅛ cup sesame oil

1. Pour boiling water over bulgur in large bowl. Set aside.
2. With steel blade in place, add dill and parsley to work bowl and process until coarsely chopped. Remove and set aside. Switch to slicing disc.
3. With slicing disc in place, pack feed tube horizontally with cucumber. Process until sliced.
4. Pack feed tube with scallions horizontally and process until sliced.
5. When all water is absorbed by bulgur, add all ingredients to it and toss well.
6. Refrigerate for at least 2 hours before serving.

YIELD: *4 servings*

Cottage Cheese Patties

Ingredients:

6 slices stale whole wheat bread (broken into pieces, or dry out fresh bread by placing in 350° oven for 5 minutes)
¼ cup walnuts
1 small onion (peeled and cut into 1-inch chunks)
1 carrot

2 eggs (lightly beaten)
1 cup cottage cheese
¼ cup butter (cut into pieces)
Salt and pepper to taste
1 teaspoon paprika
2 cups tomato sauce
1 tablespoon oil for oiling baking sheet

1. Preheat oven to 350°.
2. With steel blade, process stale bread into fine crumbs and set aside.
3. With steel blade, process walnuts until coarsely chopped. Remove to large bowl.
4. With shredding disc, shred carrots. Add to bowl.
5. With steel blade, process onion chunks until finely chopped. Add to bowl.
6. With steel blade in place, add eggs, cheese, butter, salt and pepper to taste, and paprika to work bowl. Process until blended. Remove to large bowl with nut mixture.
7. Mix ingredients in large bowl together.
8. Form into patties and roll in bread crumbs.
9. Bake in oiled baking dish 10 minutes.
10. Then pour sauce over patties. Bake 10 more minutes and serve.

YIELD: *3–4 servings*

Pizza

The Best by Cristina!

Dough Ingredients:

2½ cups unbleached flour
1 teaspoon salt
2 teaspoons dry yeast
¾ cup plus 2 tablespoons warm
   water

2 tablespoons olive oil
¼ teaspoon sugar
Cornmeal

1. With plastic blade in place, mix flour and salt in work bowl, using 3–4 1-second bursts.
2. Dissolve yeast in warm water. Stir in olive oil and sugar.
3. With processor running, gradually pour in yeast mixture and continue to process approximately 10 seconds, until dough starts to come together. It will not quite form a ball. (Note: The dough may actually look quite crumbly after processing, but will easily come together with a couple of kneading strokes. It will *definitely not* resemble a ball at the end of the processing stage—don't be alarmed when you come up with what looks like a crumbly mess!)
4. Turn onto lightly floured surface and knead briefly until smooth.
5. Shape into symmetrical ball, tucking all ends under as you work. Place on floured pizza pan and cover loosely with plastic wrap. Set on top of counter and let rise until doubled or tripled in bulk, approximately 2–2½ hours.
6. On lightly floured surface, start forming dough into pizza shape by flouring your hands and stretching the dough into a flat circle. Be careful not to compress the dough as this will ruin the texture of the crust.
7. Sprinkle pizza pan with cornmeal. Place dough on pan and pinch up ends to form a thick rim. Cover with plastic wrap and set aside.
8. While the shaped pizza is rising again, you can work on the sauce and the filling (recipes follow).

YIELD: *1 12-inch pizza, serves 4 hungry people*

Pizza Topping

The pizza topping should be prepared before the sauce. This will save cleanup time (dry ingredients before wet ingredients).

Ingredients:

½ pound mozzarella cheese
½ pound mushrooms
¼ cup grated Parmesan cheese

1 teaspoon oregano
Olive oil

1. With grating disc, grate mozzarella cheese. Set aside.
2. With slicing disc in place, slice mushrooms into medium-thick slices. Set aside.

Cristina's Pizza Sauce

Ingredients:

2 cloves garlic (peeled)
1 medium spanish onion (peeled and quartered)
2 tablespoons olive oil
1 bay leaf
1 28-ounce can stewed tomatoes
1 12-ounce can tomato sauce
¼ cup dry sherry
½ teaspoon salt
¼ teaspoon freshly ground pepper
1 teaspoon dried basil

1. Preheat oven to 425°.
2. Peel garlic. With steel blade in place, mince using 3 1-second bursts.
3. Peel onion and cut in half. Add to work bowl and chop using 4–5 1-second bursts.
4. Heat oil in skillet (I use my wok). Sauté onion and garlic with bay leaf until onion is transparent.
5. Add all other ingredients. Simmer approximately 15 minutes.
6. Purée pizza sauce as follows:
   Transfer sauce in small batches (no more than 2 cups) to bowl of processor. With steel blade in place run machine 10 seconds. Check to see if sauce is sufficiently smooth. If not, process an additional 5 seconds. Repeat until all sauce has been puréed.
7. Set aside sauce. This recipe yields 5 cups, and it is a good idea to freeze the unused portion for future use.

YIELD: *5 cups*

NOTE: Now it is time to assemble the pizza for baking. Directions follow.

Assembling the Pizza

1. Brush top of dough lightly with olive oil.
2. Spoon just enough sauce on pizza to cover the dough lightly.
3. Sprinkle on Parmesan cheese.
4. Spread sliced mushrooms on evenly.
5. Sprinkle with oregano.
6. Top with grated mozzarella cheese.
7. Bake immediately (otherwise the crust will get soggy). Place pizza on middle rack of preheated 425° oven. Bake 15–20 minutes, or until cheese is melted and crust is golden.

Cristina's Vegetarian Quiche

Ingredients:

2 9-inch pie crusts
1 medium spanish onion (peeled and root end trimmed)
2 tablespoons butter
½ pound fresh mushrooms
½ pound Gruyère cheese
4 large eggs

¾ cup milk
1 cup cream (heavy, light or half and half)
½ teaspoon salt
¼ teaspoon cayenne pepper
¼ teaspoon freshly grated nutmeg

1. Preheat oven to 450°. Bake pie crusts at 450° for 5 minutes or until just beginning to color. Remove from oven and set aside. Reduce oven temperature to 350°.
2. With slicing disc in place, add onion to feed tube. Process using light pressure on food pusher for thin slices.
3. Melt butter in large skillet. Add sliced onion and sauté over low heat while you proceed with mushrooms.
4. With slicing disc in place, pack feed tube with mushrooms. Process as for onion above. Repeat until all mushrooms are thinly sliced.
5. When onion in skillet is translucent, turn heat to high. Add mushrooms and sauté several minutes until mushrooms are golden. Remove from heat and set aside.
6. With shredding disc in place, fit Gruyère into feed tube. Process using high pressure on food pusher. Remove shredded cheese from work bowl and set aside.
7. With steel blade in place, add eggs, milk, cream, salt, pepper and nutmeg to work bowl. Process 5 seconds or until well combined.
8. Sprinkle half of the shredded cheese over bottom of each pie crust. Top with half of the onion and mushroom mixture. Pour half of the egg mixture into each crust. Bake at 350° for 35 minutes or until set and tops are golden.

YIELD: *serves 10–12*

Chapter 6

DINNER

SEAFOOD ENTRÉES

How to Choose Fresh Seafood

The fresher seafood is, the better, and there are several points to observe in its selection.

FISH:
1. The eyes should be bulging over their surfaces, bright and clear.
2. Gills should be reddish pink; they should be without slime or unnatural odor.
3. The flesh should cling close to the bones, firm and elastic to the touch. Press down—it should bounce back.
4. Scales should retain their brightly colored sheen and adhere tightly to the skin.
5. All fish has a characteristic odor, but fresh fish never has an objectionable odor.

SHELLFISH:
1. Clams, mussels and oysters are good only when alive, which is indicated by a tightly closed shell. Even slightly opened shells are not to be used.
2. Crabs and lobsters are easily identifiable by the lively movement of head and claws. They must be alive until the moment of cooking.
3. Fresh prawns and shrimp are greenish in color and firm to the touch.
4. Bay and sea scallops are marketed shucked and should have a firm white appearance when absolutely fresh.

Grilled Sea Bass with Endive

Ingredients:

4 1-inch thick sea bass steaks (about 2½ pounds)

1 sauce recipe for Cold Noodles Szechuan Style (page 118)

6 belgian endives (root ends trimmed)

¾ pound zucchini (scrubbed and ends removed)

1 tablespoon oil for cooking

2 3.5-ounce packages enoki mushrooms (root ends trimmed, or ½ pound regular mushrooms sliced)

Juice of 2 lemons

1. Place fish steaks in glass or stainless steel dish in one layer. Pour ½ cup sauce over steaks. Turn steaks to coat with sauce. Set aside to marinate for 30 minutes.
2. With slicing disc in place, pack feed tube with endives, vertically with root end toward the blade. Process with medium pressure on feed tube. Repeat until all endives are processed. Leave endive in work bowl.
3. Switch to shredding disc. Cut zucchini to fit horizontally in feed tube. Pack feed tube and process with light pressure on food pusher for fine long shreds.
4. Grill marinated fish steaks over hot coals (or 3 inches from preheated broiler) for 5–7 minutes per side. Fish is done when it flakes easily with a fork. Do *not* overcook.
5. While fish is cooking, heat 1 tablespoon oil in a wok or large skillet over medium-high heat. Add processed endive and zucchini. Stir fry 1 minute. Add mushrooms and lemon juice. Stir fry 1 minute. Remove to large warmed serving platter.
6. When fish steaks are done, place on top of vegetable mixture. Drizzle remaining sauce over all. Serve immediately.

YIELD: *4 servings*

Sesame Fish Balls

Ingredients:

½ pound shrimp (peeled)
½ pound white fish fillets (cut in 2-inch pieces)
3 scallions (trimmed and cut in 1-inch pieces)
½ bunch parsley and/or dill (rinsed, dried and stems removed)
1 large clove garlic (peeled)

2 large eggs
1 tablespoon sesame seeds
⅛ teaspoon salt
⅛ teaspoon pepper
3 cups oil for deep frying
½ cup wheat germ (or bread crumbs)
Lemon wedges

DIPPING SAUCE:

1 scallion (trimmed and cut in 1-inch pieces)
1 1-inch piece fresh ginger root (peeled)

1 large clove garlic (peeled)
¼ cup tamari
¼ cup water

1. With steel blade in place, add shrimp, fish, scallions, parsley and/or dill and garlic to work bowl. Process until mixture is finely minced but not puréed.
2. Add 1 egg, sesame seeds, salt and pepper. Process just until well combined. Form into 1-inch balls. Place on foil-covered cookie sheet and refrigerate loosely covered for 1 hour. (Recipe may be prepared in advance to this point and refrigerated up to 8 hours before cooking.)
3. While balls are chilling, prepare sauce. With steel blade in place, add scallion to work bowl. Cover and start processor. Immediately drop ginger and garlic down feed tube and process until finely minced. Stop processor. Add tamari and water. Process just to combine. Pour into small bowl, cover and refrigerate.
4. Heat oil in wok or deep fryer to 375°. In small bowl, lightly beat remaining egg. Place wheat germ on plate or in shallow bowl.
5. Dip each fish ball in beaten egg, dredge in wheat germ and carefully drop into hot oil. Fry 6 or 7 at a time until golden. Remove with slotted spoon. Place on cookie sheet lined with paper towels and keep warm in 200° oven. Repeat until all fish balls are cooked.
6. Serve hot with Dipping Sauce.

YIELD: *approximately 24 fish balls*

THE CHENAULT STORY

This recipe was created for two of my favorite people, Stanley Goodman and Linda Chenault. I was introduced to them through Stanley's brother Michael, a New York friend of mine who also happens to be my dentist. Michael kept saying that we should all meet and when we finally did, Michael was right—it was love at first sight for all of us! Linda and Stanley have been in the fashion industry for years and as we shared career stories and goals, I came to discover the incredible clothing designs of Linda Chenault, head designer for "Warren Z." They're all I've worn since! It's made dressing for all the seasons so simple because all the clothes are so well coordinated. Just a few pieces can be turned into a complete wardrobe. I've worn Linda's "Warren Z" creations all over the world and the response was the same everywhere—people love them.

In appreciation, I designed this recipe for them, hoping to please their artistic sense as well as their appetite. I hope they—and you—enjoy it as much as I've enjoyed Chenault!

Cashew Ginger Shrimp à la Chenault

Ingredients:

Hot cooked brown rice
1 small bunch dill (stems removed)
2 cloves garlic (peeled)
1 2-inch piece ginger (peeled)
2 scallions (ends trimmed and cut into 2-inch pieces)
1¼ pounds fresh shrimp (peeled and rinsed)
⅛ teaspoon cayenne pepper

⅛ teaspoon turmeric
1¼ cups milk
1 onion (peeled)
2 tablespoons oil
2 tablespoons lime juice
1 teaspoon honey
¼ cup raw cashew pieces
1 tablespoon cornstarch
1½ teaspoons salt

1. Prepare the rice according to the recipe on page 117. When done, set aside.
2. Meanwhile, with steel blade in place, add dill to work bowl. With motor running, drop garlic cloves and ginger through feed tube. Process until finely minced.
3. Stop machine. Remove cover and add scallions to work bowl. Process until coarsely chopped.
4. In large skillet, combine shrimp, scallion mixture, cayenne, turmeric and 1 cup milk. Cover and simmer 6–8 minutes depending on size.
5. With slicing disc in place, pack feed tube with onion and process until sliced.
6. Heat oil in small skillet and sauté onion slices until tender. Add lime juice, honey and cashews and stir.
7. Dissolve cornstarch in ¼ cup milk and pour into shrimp mixture. Stir.
8. Add sautéed onion and salt, stir, and cook until thickened.
9. Serve over hot brown rice. (Rice will stay warm a long time, but if you need to reheat it, do so gently over a low flame for 5 minutes, covered.)

YIELD: *4 servings*

Seafood Falafel with Cucumber Sauce

Ingredients:

FALAFEL:

½ pound dried chickpeas (rinsed)
1 large onion (peeled and quartered)
2 1-inch pieces fresh ginger root (peeled and quartered)
1 bunch parsley (rinsed, dried and stems removed)
3 large cloves garlic (peeled)
½ pound cod, turbot or other white fish fillet (cut in 2-inch pieces)

1½ teaspoons ground coriander
1½ teaspoons ground cumin
1 teaspoon salt
½ teaspoon cayenne pepper
½ teaspoon baking powder
1 large egg (lightly beaten)
2 tablespoons milk
1 tablespoon Dijon mustard
1–1½ cups fine dry bread crumbs (whole wheat is best)
Oil for baking trays

CUCUMBER SAUCE:

1 large cucumber (peeled, seeded and cut in 2-inch pieces)
½ bunch parsley (rinsed, dried and stems removed)
1 large scallion (trimmed and cut in 1-inch pieces)

1 large clove garlic (peeled)
1½ cups plain yogurt
1 teaspoon celery seed
½ teaspoon salt
¼ teaspoon cayenne pepper

1. Cook chickpeas according to package directions until tender. While peas are cooking, prepare Cucumber Sauce.
2. In work bowl fitted with steel blade, place cucumber, parsley and scallion. Lock cover and start processor. Immediately drop garlic clove down feed tube and process 3 seconds. Stop processor, remove cover and scrape down sides of work bowl with spatula. Replace cover and process with several 1-second bursts until mixture is finely minced.
3. Remove cover. Add yogurt, celery seed, salt and cayenne pepper. Lock cover in place and process with 3–4 1-second bursts just to combine ingredients. Pour sauce into bowl, cover and refrigerate. Replace unwashed work bowl fitted with steel blade on base.
4. In work bowl place quartered onion, quartered ginger root and parsley. Lock cover in place and start processor. Immediately drop garlic cloves down feed tube and process 3 seconds. Stop processor, remove cover and scrape down sides of bowl. Replace cover and process with 5–6 1-second bursts until mixture is finely minced. Scrape mixture into large bowl and set aside.
5. Replace work bowl fitted with steel blade on base. Add fish, lock cover and process until fish is finely minced but not puréed. Scrape fish into bowl with onion mixture. Replace work bowl and steel blade on base.
6. When chickpeas are tender, drain in colander and rinse with cold water to cool. Drain well.

7. Purée chickpeas in processor. You may have to do this in several batches depending on the capacity of your work bowl. Add puréed chickpeas to fish and onion mixture.
8. Add coriander, cumin, salt, cayenne and baking powder to the purée mixture. Combine well.
9. In small bowl combine beaten egg, milk and mustard; place bread crumbs in shallow bowl or on a plate.
10. Form purée mixture into balls (see Yield). Dip each ball into egg mixture, dredge in bread crumbs and arrange 1-inch apart on well-oiled baking trays or cookie sheets. Refrigerate for 1 hour, loosely covered. (Note: Recipe may be prepared in advance to this point. Refrigerate loosely covered up to 8 hours or place trays in freezer and freeze until hard. Transfer to plastic bags or airtight freezer containers and keep frozen up to 2 weeks.)
11. Preheat oven to 375°. Bake falafel for 20 minutes or until golden brown.
12. Serve appetizer-size falafel on picks. Arrange on tray surrounding a bowl of Cucumber Sauce. As a main course, serve 2–3 large falafel per person with a bit of the sauce spooned over them. Serve additional sauce on the side.

YIELD: *18 2½-inch balls or 48 appetizer-size balls*

Maryland Crab Cakes

Having lived in Maryland for many years, I discovered that one of the local treasures there is crabs. The Chesapeake Bay is filled with them and just about anywhere you go, hot steamed crabs, crab cakes and ice cold beer are sure to be found on the menu. This recipe for them is my favorite.

Ingredients:

2 slices whole wheat bread
¼ cup milk
1 pound crabmeat (backfin is best)
A few sprigs fresh parsley (rinsed, dried and stems removed)
1 teaspoon sesame seeds

1 egg
1 tablespoon mayonnaise
1 tablespoon Dijon mustard
1 teaspoon Worcestershire sauce
Salt and pepper to taste
1 cup oil for cooking

GARNISH:
Parsley
Paprika
Lemon wedges

1. Dip bread in milk and break into small pieces. Set aside.
2. Place crabmeat in bowl and go through with fingers to remove any shells (frozen crabmeat is best rinsed first under cold water to remove metallic taste).
3. With steel blade in place, add parsley to work bowl and process until coarsely chopped. Stop machine.
4. Add all other ingredients to work bowl and process to combine.
5. Heat oil in large skillet.
6. Form batter into 6 patties.
7. Fry until golden on both sides.
8. Serve garnished with parsley and lemon wedges, and sprinkled with paprika.

YIELD: *6 cakes*

Judy's Spinach Pasta with Tofu Clam Sauce

When I met Jimmy Glenn it was a pleasure and a privilege to find a friend I could collaborate with—both in the kitchen and on paper. Little did I know that when I met his parents, Jim and Judy Glenn, I would also find two more collaborators. Jim taught me how to make the best chili ever and Judy tests and creates recipes for all my books now.

This next one is really special. I wanted to find a way to have the taste and texture of a creamy cheese Alfredo sauce without the overwhelming richness and calorie count. Judy experimented with Skip and me and we perfected the use of tofu to create such a sauce. It's creamy and delicious and, without all the butter, cream and cheese, it's healthy and light. Its only decadence is in the fabulous flavor!

Ingredients:

3 dozen fresh clams	½ cup cilantro leaves
1 cup dry white wine	3 large cloves garlic (peeled)
1 teaspoon oregano	8 ounces tofu (drained and
½ teaspoon crushed red pepper	pressed)
3 large scallions (trimmed and cut	1 pound spinach pasta
in 1-inch pieces)	4 tablespoons olive oil
1 bunch dill (stems removed)	

1. Steam clams in wine until open. Drain clams, reserving cooking liquid. Strain liquid through several thicknesses of cheesecloth into small saucepan. Remove clams from shells and set aside.
2. To reserved cooking liquid, add oregano and crushed red pepper. Bring to boil and cook over medium heat until reduced in volume to 1 cup.
3. While liquid is reducing, prepare tofu sauce base. To work bowl fitted with steel blade, add scallions, dill, cilantro leaves and 20 of the cooked clams. Lock cover and start machine. Immediately drop garlic down feed tube. Process 3 seconds. Stop machine and scrape down side of work bowl with spatula. Cover and process for several-second bursts until ingredients are finely chopped. Scrape into small bowl and set aside.
4. With steel blade in place, crumble tofu into work bowl. Lock cover and process until tofu is smooth and creamy. With processor running, pour reduced clam liquid down feed tube in steady stream. Process 5 seconds. Pour tofu mixture into same saucepan used to reduce clam liquid. Stir in chopped greens. Cover and heat over low heat.
5. Cook spinach pasta al dente. Drain. Toss pasta with olive oil. Pour hot tofu clam sauce over pasta. Toss well.
6. Serve on warm plates or bowls. Garnish with remaining 16 whole clams.

YIELD: *4 servings*

Baked Fish Burgers

Ingredients:

½ bunch dill (stems removed)
½ bunch fresh parsley (stems removed)
1 onion (peeled and quartered)
1 stalk celery (trimmed and cut in 1-inch pieces)
2 pounds fillet of haddock or cod
2 carrots (well scrubbed)

½ teaspoon salt
⅛ teaspoon black pepper
1 egg (lightly beaten)
2 teaspoons Dijon mustard
½ cup water
1 teaspoon oil
½ cup boiling water

SAUCE:

1 cup mayonnaise
¼ cup Dijon mustard
2 tablespoons horseradish

2 tablespoons chopped parsley and dill (reserved from above)

1. Preheat oven to 350°.
2. With steel blade in place, add dill and parsley to work bowl. Cover and process for 3–4 1-second bursts until finely chopped. Remove 2 tablespoons of the mixture and reserve for sauce. Remove the remainder to a 2-quart bowl.
3. With steel blade in place, add onion and celery to work bowl. Cover and process until finely chopped. Remove to bowl with chopped herbs.
4. With steel blade in place, add fish fillets to work bowl. Cover and process until finely ground. Remove to bowl with herbs and vegetables.
5. With shredding disc in place, pack feed tube with carrots vertically. Process with light pressure on feed tube to make thin shreds. Remove to bowl with ground fish.
6. To above mixture, add salt, pepper, egg, mustard and the ½ cup water. Combine well.
7. Grease a casserole dish or roasting pan with oil. Shape fish mixture into balls using about ½ cup of the mixture per ball. Place in greased casserole in single layer.
8. Bake at 350° for 15 minutes. Add ½ cup boiling water to casserole to prevent sticking and bake 30 minutes more or until golden.
9. While fish balls are baking, add all sauce ingredients to work bowl fitted with steel blade. Cover and process 3 seconds just to combine.
10. Pour sauce into bowl and serve at room temperature with hot fish balls.

Variation:

For crispy fish balls, roll in bread crumbs. Grease casserole with 1 tablespoon oil and omit 1 cup boiling water during baking.

YIELD: *4 servings*

FROM RUSSELL BENNETT'S KITCHEN

It is once again a privilege to include in my book recipes from Russell Bennett, a dear friend and co-author of my second book, *Recipe for a Great Affair: How to Cater Your Own Party or Anybody Else's!* Russell is a top caterer in New York City, so into his kitchens we went to collaborate on new ideas for the food processor and more great recipes for you!

Scallop Stuffed Mushrooms

This is a great one for company! It can be made ahead of time and heated just before serving.

Ingredients:

4 shallot cloves (peeled)
1 large clove garlic (peeled)
2 cups white table wine
16 large mushrooms (stems removed and reserved)
½ pound *baby bay* scallops (the *very* tiny ones, or you can use larger *bay* scallops halved)

1 tablespoon butter
¼ bunch fresh dill (rinsed, dried and stems removed)
½ teaspoon salt
⅛ teaspoon pepper
3 tablespoons pignoli nuts
Sprinkle of paprika (about ¼ teaspoon)

1. With steel blade in place, turn machine on and drop shallots and garlic through feed tube. Process until coarsely chopped.
2. Place 2 cups wine in large covered skillet.
3. Add shallots and garlic to wine and bring to boil.
4. Add mushrooms and spoon wine mixture over them. Reduce heat, cover and poach 4 minutes.
5. Remove mushrooms from pan to bowl. Set aside.
6. Add scallops to wine mixture. Bring to boil, cover, lower heat and poach 4 minutes. Then remove to plate.
7. With steel blade in place, add mushroom stems to work bowl and process until finely chopped.
8. Add butter to liquid remaining in skillet. Add chopped stems. Bring to boil and reduce until mixture has thickened, then turn off heat.
9. With steel blade in place, add dill to work bowl and process until finely chopped.
10. Stir dill into mushroom mixture with salt and pepper.
11. Add scallops and pignoli nuts to skillet and stir to combine with heat turned *off*.
12. Spoon mixture into reserved caps. Place on baking pan and sprinkle lightly with paprika.
13. When ready to serve: Place room temperature mushrooms in pre-heated 350° oven for 5 minutes. (They also heat well and very quickly in a microwave.)

YIELD: *4 servings*

VEGETARIAN ENTRÉES

Pasta with Tofu Spinach Pesto Sauce

In the midst of experimenting with recipes for my books, I get so overwhelmed by the possibilities I literally start dreaming about food! I wake up excited to try what haunted my sleep. This is one of those night-time visions. I love pesto and think it's something for every cook to be familiar with because it's so tasty on many things, from pasta to seafood. In my dream, I envisioned a pesto without all the cheese and much less oil—a pesto that could be enjoyed often without feeling guilty about calories. Well, this is it—it worked! Instead of cheese, I used tofu, which purées to a creamy consistency and needs less oil than traditional pesto.

Ingredients:

3 large cloves garlic (peeled)
1 pound fresh spinach (tough stems removed and washed well)
1 cup fresh basil leaves (washed well)
½ cup pignoli nuts
½ teaspoon salt
½ teaspoon freshly ground pepper
1 pound tofu (drained, squeezed and crumbled)
½ cup olive oil
1 pound pasta (cooked al dente)
1 dozen cherry tomatoes (halved)

1. With steel blade in place, drop garlic down feed tube with the motor running, and process until finely minced.
2. Add spinach and basil to work bowl. Process until puréed.
3. Add pignoli, salt, pepper, and tofu. Process until smooth and creamy.
4. With motor running slowly, add oil through feed tube and process until well combined.
5. Pour sauce into top half of double boiler. Cover and place over hot but not boiling water until sauce is warmed through. Stir occasionally.
6. To serve: Toss hot, drained pasta with warm sauce and tomato halves.

YIELD: *4 servings*

NOTE: Sauce is also great, warm or cold, as a dip for vegetables or spooned over fish.

Grandma's Zucchini and Pasta

Here comes another one of Grandma Anastasio's . . . If I had to pick one meal to eat every day forever, it would have to be this one! Crispy fried zucchini tossed with hot buttered spaghetti and topped with Parmesan cheese—what could be better? It's easy and it's inexpensive. Don't be surprised if it becomes part of your own standard repertoire!

Ingredients:

2 scallions (ends trimmed and cut into 2-inch lengths)
2 cloves garlic (peeled)
2–3 yellow squash or zucchini (or any combination of the two; washed, ends removed and cut into lengths to fit your feed tube)
Olive oil for cooking
Salt and pepper to taste
½ teaspoon dried basil
¾ cup grated Parmesan cheese
¼ cup butter (melted)
½ pound pasta

1. With steel blade in place, add scallions to work bowl, cover and process. With motor running, drop garlic through feed tube. Process until coarsely chopped. Stop machine, empty work bowl and set aside.
2. Switch to slicing disc. Pack feed tube with zucchini and process to produce thin circles. Remove to plate and set aside.
3. Put salted water to boil and cook spaghetti al dente according to directions. Drain well when ready.
4. Heat wok or large frying pan, necklace with oil and sauté zucchini in batches, sprinkling each batch with salt and pepper, removing to plate as ready, until crisp and golden, adding oil as necessary.
5. Add scallion and garlic and basil to frying pan or wok and sauté until golden; add all the zucchini back to frying pan or wok. Toss and combine, cover and turn off heat.
6. Toss drained pasta with melted butter and ½ cup cheese.
7. Zucchini can be tossed with pasta or pasta can be portioned on each plate and topped with zucchini. Serve with additional Parmesan cheese.

YIELD: *2 servings*

Cristina's Enchiladas Verdes

(Green Enchiladas)

This is adapted from an old family recipe as served in Mexico City. These enchiladas are mild and delicious.

Ingredients:

6 tomatillos (see note)

18 fresh California chilies (roasted, peeled and seeded, or 1 26-ounce can green California chilies drained)

⅓ cup fresh cilantro (stems removed)

1 cup water

2 tablespoons olive oil

½ teaspoon salt

2 tablespoons olive oil for cooking tortillas

1 dozen flour or corn tortillas (see note)

1 pound jack cheese

½ cup sour cream

2 tablespoons milk

1. Blanch tomatillos in boiling water for 2–3 minutes. Rinse in cold water, peel and cut into halves. Add to work bowl fitted with steel blade along with chilies and cilantro. Cover and process 10 seconds. Stop processor and scrape down sides of work bowl. If mixture is not smooth, process several seconds more.
2. Add water, olive oil and salt to chili mixture. Process 5 seconds until well combined.
3. Pour into a 2-quart saucepan and simmer over medium heat 15 minutes. Remove from heat, strain and set aside. Yields about 1 quart enchilada sauce.
4. Preheat oven to 350°. Heat oil for cooking in a non-stick skillet. Fry tortillas one at a time by holding with tongs and dipping in hot oil for 30 seconds on each side. Drain on paper towels. It is important that tortillas not be overcooked. If you fry them too long, they will become crisp and hard to work with. You want them to remain soft and pliable.
5. With shredding disc in place, load feed tube with jack cheese trimmed to fit tube snugly. Shred, using light pressure on food pusher. Reserve ¼ cup shredded cheese for garnish.
6. Ladle some of the enchilada sauce into a shallow bowl. Using tongs, dip a tortilla into sauce coating both sides. Remove from sauce, place 2 heaping tablespoons shredded cheese in center and roll tortilla into a cylinder, enclosing cheese. Place seam side down in a rectangular baking dish. Repeat with remaining tortillas and place in single layer in baking dish.
7. Pour remaining enchilada sauce over rolled tortillas. Combine sour cream and milk. Pour over enchilada sauce. Sprinkle with reserved shredded cheese.

8. Bake at 350° for 30 minutes or until heated through and cheese is melted.

Goes well with rice, red beans and a tossed green salad.

YIELD: *4–6 servings*

NOTE: A tomatillo is a small yellow-green fruit that resembles a tomato, available fresh in Spanish and Mexican markets.

Tortillas are available in the frozen food section of most markets—Cristina prefers *flour*.

Skip's Pasta Impromptu

For one of our testing sessions, we packed our things and went to Ocean City, Maryland, for some springtime weather at the beach. By the time we arrived there were 50 m.p.h. winds and snow in the forecast. It was already late evening when Skip confessed to a pasta craving that *had* to be satisfied! Not wanting to brave the icy ocean chill, into the kitchen he went, emerging a half hour later with Pasta Impromptu. I might not have been in the mood to cook that night but it didn't prevent me from devouring his delicious "midnight snack!" Pasta seems to be a universal favorite, and when you use imported or fresh pasta and lots of vegetables, it's healthy and not as fattening as you might think . . . so, enjoy! Enjoy!

Ingredients:

¼ pound mushrooms (brushed clean)
2 large scallions (ends removed; cut into 2-inch lengths)
2 large cloves garlic (peeled)
1 cup stemmed parsley (rinsed and dried)
1 medium tomato (cored and quartered)

½ cup olive oil
4 ounces beer
¼ teaspoon salt
½ teaspoon basil
¼ teaspoon thyme
¼ teaspoon red pepper flakes
½ pound very thin spaghetti

1. With slicing disc in place, pack the feed tube with the mushrooms and process with light pressure on food pusher. Repeat until all mushrooms are processed. Remove and set aside.
2. With steel blade in place, add scallions to work bowl and process. With machine running, drop in garlic through feed tube. Process until coarsely chopped. Remove and set aside.
3. With steel blade in place, add parsley to work bowl and process until coarsely chopped. Remove and set aside.
4. With steel blade in place, add tomato to work bowl. Process until coarsely chopped. Remove to bowl with parsley and set aside.
5. Heat ½ cup oil in wok or frying pan. Put scallion and garlic mixture into it. Sauté over medium heat, stirring, for 2 minutes.
6. Turn heat up to high and add mushrooms. Sauté until they are golden, stirring constantly.
7. Add beer and spices and stir to mix well. Simmer over low heat for 7–10 minutes.
8. Meanwhile, prepare pasta according to directions, al dente.
9. When pasta is almost cooked, add chopped tomato and parsley to mushrooms and heat through.
10. Drain pasta and pour sauce over top. Enjoy!

YIELD: *2 servings*

MEAT AND POULTRY ENTRÉES

GRIND YOUR OWN MEATS AND POULTRY . . .

Chop, slice and shred them, too! Here's an opportunity to let your food processor give you a greater value for the money you spend on meat. Average prices today for a good quality ground round or sirloin approach $3.00 a pound. Watch for supermarket specials on boneless top round or sirloin tip roasts. They are often sale-priced as much as $1.00 per pound less than ground sirloin. Buy two 3-pound packages. Oven or pot roast one and save any leftovers for Hollywood Minced Beef Salad (page 102). From the second, cut a 3-inch thick slice and reserve for Skip's Sukiyaki (page 100). Cut the remainder of the second roast into 1-inch cubes, trimming away any gristle or membrane. Use for Steak Tartare (page 49) or elegant and simple Sesame Beef Kabobs (page 99). My local butcher recently featured sirloin tip roasts at $1.99 per pound. I bought 2 3-pound roasts for just under $12.00. By following the suggestions listed above, I served two dinners for 4, one brunch for 4 and one late supper for 6. That amounted to main courses for 18 hungry people costing under $20.00. Now that's what I call value! And my food processor made it easy and elegant as well.

HINTS FOR PROCESSING MEATS AND POULTRY

1. Follow your processor's instruction manual as to quantities of meat your machine can handle at one time. Never exceed them or your machine will overheat and stall.
2. Trim all bone, gristle, membrane and fat from meat (and skin as well from poultry) before processing. For chopping or grinding, cut meat into 1-inch cubes. For slicing or shredding, cut meat to fit tightly in the feed tube of your machine.
3. Raw beef, lamb, veal, pork or poultry should be *well chilled* for chopping or grinding and *partially frozen* for slicing or shredding.
4. For chopping or grinding, add well-chilled cubed meat to work bowl fitted with steel blade. Process with on/off bursts until desired consistency is reached. For slicing or shredding with the appropriate disc in place, pack feed tube tightly with partially frozen meat. Use medium to firm pressure on food pusher.
5. When chopping meat for burgers or pâtés, I find that a 2-to-1 proportion of meat to fat gives the most flavorful and juicy results. Save any fat when trimming meat and poultry, cut it into 1-inch pieces and process with the meat.
6. Follow the same hints for processing cooked meats. For slicing or shredding it may not be necessary to freeze the meat partially if cooking has made it firm, as with chicken. Simply have it well chilled before packing the feed tube, and use light to medium pressure on the food pusher when processing.

Grandma Anastasio's Lasagna

My Grandmother Anastasio insisted on the best ingredients available and would walk all over New York for the *best* cheese, the *freshest* vegetables and the *finest* meats. She trained my young eyes to select the ripest, most perfect of everything. It was an invaluable lesson. She never seemed to mind my endless questions and constant observation of her technique. Much to my delight, days spent in her kitchen invariably ended with plates of her luscious concoctions. I only wish she might have lived long enough to see how well her lessons were learned and how many people all over the country would benefit from the knowledge she passed down to me.

Grandma never used a food processor for her lasagna, but I'm sure she would have if they'd been available in her day!

Ingredients:

3 cloves garlic
½ bunch fresh parsley (rinsed, dried and stems removed)
1 large onion (peeled and quartered)
1 28-ounce can Italian plum tomatoes
½ pound pepperoni
1 pound fresh mushrooms
2 pounds sweet sausage
¼ cup olive oil
1 tablespoon sweet basil
1 heaping teaspoon oregano
2 large bay leaves

1 28-ounce can tomato purée
2 small cans tomato paste
1½ cups fresh grated Parmesan or Romano cheese
1 cup red wine
1 13-ounce can chicken stock (or 2 cups homemade stock)
1 teaspoon sugar
2 pounds ricotta cheese
1 egg (lightly beaten)
2 pounds very cold mozzarella
1 pound lasagna noodles (try spinach or whole wheat noodles—they're great!)

1. With steel blade in place and motor running, drop peeled garlic cloves down feed tube. Process until minced, remove and set aside.
2. With steel blade in place, add parsley to work bowl. Process until finely chopped, remove and set aside.
3. With steel blade in place, put quartered onion in work bowl. Process until coarsely chopped, remove and set aside.
4. With steel blade in place, add Italian plum tomatoes to work bowl. Process only until coarsely chopped. Set aside.
5. Clean work bowl. Switch to slicing blade. Pack feed tube with pepperoni and with light pressure on food pusher, process until sliced. Remove and set aside.
6. Pack feed tube with mushrooms and process until sliced. Remove and set aside.
7. Cut sausage into 1-inch pieces.
8. Heat olive oil in heavy saucepot and brown sausage and pepperoni.
9. Add garlic, basil, oregano, bay leaf, mushrooms and onions. Cover and cook over low heat for 5 minutes.

10. Add tomatoes, purée, paste, half the parsley, ½ cup Parmesan cheese, wine, stock and sugar.
11. Stir and simmer, covered, over low heat at least 1 hour (or make sauce the day before and refrigerate).
12. Meanwhile, mix ricotta in small bowl with remaining parsley and egg. Set aside.
13. With shredding disc in place, shred cold mozzarella cheese. Remove and set aside.
14. Make lasagna noodles al dente according to directions and drain well.
15. To assemble lasagna, use 1 ladle of sauce and one layer of noodles followed by a layer of ricotta, mozzarella, sauce and more noodles until all ingredients are used. Top with more sauce and the rest of the Parmesan.
16. Bake 45 minutes in a 350° oven. Serve with additional sauce.

YIELD: *6 servings*

Aunt Jean's German Noodles and Cabbage

This recipe was initially published in my first cookbook, *Getting into Your Wok with Annette Annechild*. It was a tremendous hit, so I have adapted it to the food processor and included it here. Aunt Jean and Uncle John still make it for me (on request) each time I visit. The ritual began when I stayed with them many years ago. I came to New York as a budding starlet, soon became a starving actress, and never appreciated a home-cooked meal more than in that period of my life. I fell in love with noodles and cabbage for its unusual flavor and with Aunt Jean and Uncle John for helping me get through my hard beginning in New York City.

Ingredients:

4 pounds cabbage (outer leaves removed, cored and cut into 2-inch wedges, or to fit your feed tube tightly)

½ teaspoon salt plus salt to taste

4 slices (nitrite free) bacon

½ pound sweet butter

Pepper to taste

1 pound wide egg noodles

1. With slicing disc in place, load feed tube with cabbage and process with moderate pressure on food pusher. Repeat until all cabbage is sliced and remove to large bowl. Toss with ½ teaspoon salt and set aside for ½ hour (or overnight stored in refrigerator).
2. Dice bacon and sauté in large pot or wok over low heat until browned.
3. When bacon is browned, add butter.
4. Squeeze excess water from cabbage and add to pot or wok, mixing with bacon and butter.
5. Add salt and pepper to taste. Simmer covered 1 hour, stirring occasionally.
6. Cook noodles as directed al dente. Drain and combine with cabbage.
7. Remove pot or wok from heat and set aside. Aunt Jean says, "The longer it sits, the better it is!"
8. Reheat over low flame if necessary and enjoy!

YIELD: *a potful!*

Sesame Beef Kabobs

Ingredients:

2 large oranges (peeled and sectioned; membranes removed)

2 teaspoons crumbled marjoram leaves

2 cucumbers (peeled, seeded and cut in 1-inch cubes)

1 3-inch piece fresh horseradish (peeled and cut in 1-inch pieces)

1 3-inch piece fresh ginger root (peeled and cut in 1-inch pieces)

2 scallions (trimmed and cut in 1-inch pieces)

2 large cloves garlic (peeled)

Zest from half an orange (cut in strips)

1½ pounds top round or sirloin tip beef (ground)

½ cup toasted sesame seeds

¼ cup tamari

2 tablespoons sesame oil (plus 2 tablespoons vegetable oil for cooking of appetizers)

Skewers or appetizer picks

1. With steel blade in place, add orange sections and marjoram to work bowl. Process until liquified. Place cucumber cubes in glass or stainless bowl. Pour liquified oranges over cubes and set aside to marinate.

2. With steel blade in place, add horseradish, ginger, scallions, garlic and orange zest to work bowl. Process with on/off bursts until finely minced. Remove to 2-quart bowl.

3. To minced ingredients, add ground beef, sesame seeds, tamari and sesame oil. Combine well.

4. For *main course* servings: Divide mixture into 12 equal portions. Shape each into a ball. Place on platter and refrigerate 1 hour.
   For *appetizers:* Shape mixture into 1-inch balls. Place on platter and refrigerate 1 hour.
   (Recipe may be prepared to this point up to 8 hours in advance, covered with plastic wrap and refrigerated.)

5. *For main course servings:* Use 4 skewers. For each skewer use 3 meat balls and 8 cucumber cubes, beginning and ending with 2 cucumber cubes. Grill over hot fire or broil 3 inches from heat source, turning skewers several times, about 8 minutes or until meat is golden and sizzling but still pink inside.
   For appetizers: Heat 1 tablespoon of the cooking oil in wok or large skillet over medium-high heat. Stir fry about 10 balls at a time until golden. Remove to plate and keep warm in 200° oven. Stir fry remaining balls. For each appetizer pick, use 2 cucumber cubes and 1 beef ball. Keep appetizers warm in a chafing dish or on a warming tray.

YIELD: *4 main course or 30 appetizer servings*

Skip's Sukiyaki

Sukiyaki is prepared by stir frying meats and vegetables separately and arranging them individually around a mound of rice. It's a highly visual and delectable dish which originated in Japan. It is actually very simple to prepare, so don't let the length of the recipe scare you off!

Ingredients:

1 pound boneless top round or sirloin tip roast (partially frozen)
½ pound mushrooms (wiped to remove grit or soil)
2 sweet red peppers (cored, seeded and halved)
1 pound bok choy (trimmed and cut to fit feed tube)
2 large carrots (scrubbed and trimmed)
2 large scallions (trimmed and cut in 1-inch pieces)

2 large cloves garlic (peeled)
1 2-inch piece fresh ginger root (peeled and halved)
Oil for stir frying
4 cups cooked brown rice (recipe page 117)
1 tablespoon sesame oil
½ pound snowpeas (stems removed)
1 pound spinach (washed well, drained and tough stems removed)

SAUCE:

¾ cup beef broth
¼ cup tamari
3 tablespoons dry sherry

2 tablespoons Toasted Almond Butter (page 64)
2 teaspoons hot chili oil

1. With slicing disc in place, load feed tube with partially frozen beef. Process with medium pressure on food pusher for thin slices. Remove to plate or bowl and set aside.
2. With slicing disc in place, pack feed tube with mushrooms. Process with light pressure on food pusher for thin slices. Repeat until all mushrooms are sliced. Remove to plate or bowl and set aside.
3. With slicing disc in place, place red pepper halves, one or two at a time, in feed tube. Process for thin slices. Repeat until all peppers are sliced. Remove to plate or bowl and set aside.
4. Replace slicing disc with shredding disc. Pack feed tube with bok choy pieces horizontally and process for long shreds. Repeat until all bok choy is shredded. Remove to bowl and set aside.
5. With shredding disc in place, load feed tube with carrots, cut to fit horizontally, and process for long shreds. Repeat until all carrots are shredded. Combine with shredded bok choy and set aside.
6. Replace shredding disc with steel blade and add scallions to work bowl. Cover and start processor. Immediately drop garlic and ginger root down feed tube. Process until finely minced. Remove to small bowl and set aside.

(Recipe may be prepared to this point several hours in advance. Cover each plate or bowl of ingredients and refrigerate until ready to cook.)

Final Preparation:

1 hour before serving time, put brown rice on to cook. In small bowl, combine beef broth, tamari, sherry, nut butter and chili oil. Set aside.

7. To proceed with Sukiyaki, 20 minutes before serving time preheat oven to 200°. Place large ovenproof serving platter and dinner plates in oven to warm. Remove all Sukiyaki ingredients from refrigerator.
8. In wok or large skillet, heat sesame oil. Add scallion, garlic and ginger mixture and stir fry 1 minute. Add beef broth mixture. Bring to the boil and simmer 1 minute. Remove to small saucepan and keep warm over low heat.
9. Heat 1 tablespoon cooking oil in same wok or skillet over high heat. When oil is almost smoking, add sliced beef. Stir fry several minutes until meat is lightly browned, but still pink inside. Add 1 tablespoon of the sauce and toss quickly to coat beef. Remove beef with skimmer or slotted spatula to warm serving platter. Keep warm in oven.
10. Add a bit more cooking oil to wok or skillet if necessary. Do not remove any juices left from stir frying meat. Add bok choy and carrot mixture and stir fry several minutes until vegetables are crisp-tender. Remove mixture from wok or skillet and add to serving platter. Pour any liquid remaining in wok over bok choy mixture. Return platter to oven.
11. Add 1 tablespoon cooking oil to wok or skillet using high heat. Add snow peas and stir fry 1 minute until bright green and crisp-tender. Remove to serving platter and return platter to oven.
12. Stir fry mushrooms over high heat just until they begin to color. Remove to serving platter and return platter to oven.
13. Add a bit more cooking oil to wok or skillet if necessary. Stir fry sliced peppers over high heat 1 minute or until crisp-tender. Remove to serving platter and return platter to oven.
14. Add spinach to wok or skillet. Sprinkle with 2 or 3 tablespoons of the sauce. Toss briefly, cover and steam 1 minute over high heat until spinach just begins to wilt. Uncover, turn off heat and remove spinach to serving platter.
15. Spoon cooked brown rice into center of serving platter. Sprinkle half of the remaining sauce over all the ingredients on the platter. Transfer remaining sauce to a small bowl.
16. Set out warmed dinner plates and place Sukiyaki platter in the center of the table. Allow guests to serve themselves and pass the remaining sauce.

YIELD: *4–6 servings*

Hollywood Minced Beef Salad

When a New Yorker goes to Hollywood, it can be an unsettling experience. (Where are the taxis? The subways? The sidewalks filled with people?) Good friends in town can change all that and turn the experience into fun and laughter.

Melody and Bob Celecia did that for me. Their warm hospitality, guidance and encouragement helped me fall in love with L.A. This next dish is one of their favorites that we've enjoyed often in the California sun.

Ingredients:

2 large potatoes (cooked until fork-tender, peeled and chilled)
½ cup Simple Garlic Vinaigrette (page 29)
2 firm ripe tomatoes (cored)
1 pound cooked roast beef (cut in 1-inch cubes and chilled)
½ bunch parsley (rinsed, dried and stems removed)

6–8 cornichons
1 clove garlic (peeled)
1 cup mung bean sprouts
½ cup Tofu "Mayonnaise" (page 27)
4 tablespoons freshly grated horseradish
1 teaspoon salt
12 large lettuce leaves
⅔ cup heavy whipping cream

GARNISH:
Additional cornichons

1. With slicing disc in place, put potato in feed tube. Process using light pressure on food pusher for thin slices. Repeat with second potato. Remove potato slices to plate or shallow bowl. Pour ¼ cup of the vinaigrette over slices. Cover and refrigerate.
2. Repeat above procedure with tomatoes, pouring remaining vinaigrette over tomato slices. Cover and refrigerate.
3. Replace slicing disc with steel blade. Process cubed beef 1 cup at a time until coarsely minced. Remove to 2-quart bowl and set aside. Repeat until all beef is minced.
4. With steel blade in place, add parsley and cornichons to work bowl. Cover and start processor. Immediately drop garlic down feed tube. Process briefly until mixture is finely minced. Add to minced beef.
5. To beef mixture add mung bean sprouts, Tofu "Mayonnaise," horseradish and salt. Combine well, cover and refrigerate 1 hour. (Recipe may be prepared to this point up to a day in advance.)
6. To proceed, 30 minutes before serving time place clean work bowl and steel blade in refrigerator to chill. Line four plates with lettuce leaves. Arrange alternating slices of marinated tomato and potato on lettuce leaves in a semicircle covering ⅔ of the perimeter of each plate.
7. Just before serving, whip cream in chilled work bowl fitted with chilled steel blade. As soon as cream begins to hold its shape, process with several more on/off bursts until cream holds firm peaks.
8. Quickly but thoroughly fold whipped cream into beef mixture. Spoon one fourth of the mixture into the center of each plate. Garnish with additional cornichons and serve immediately.

YIELD: *4 servings*

Lyda's Favorite Tiger Stew

No, this one doesn't have tiger on the ingredients list! It's actually just a favorite of the Tigers'—Clemson Tigers, that is. Clemson is a small town in South Carolina that is the home of Clemson University and the 1982 football champions, the Clemson Tigers. I've never seen any town so devoted to their team as these Tiger fans—practically everything in the town is orange in honor of them. Giant Tiger paw prints even decorate the highway into town, alerting travelers that they are indeed in Tiger Country. The Glenn family are avid fans, led by Lyda Glenn, who's been supporting the team for decades.

This recipe was created for dedicated sports fans everywhere to enjoy at a victory dinner party!

Ingredients:

2 pounds boned chuck (cut in 2-inch cubes)	2 large carrots (scrubbed and cut in 2-inch lengths)
½ pound lean pork (cut in 2-inch cubes)	1 rutabaga (cut to fit feed tube)
5 teaspoons salt	2 onions (peeled and quartered)
½ teaspoon black pepper	2 large celery stalks (cut in 3-inch lengths)
½ teaspoon turmeric	2 sweet potatoes
½ teaspoon oregano	¾–1 pound cabbage (cut in wedges)
1 bay leaf	3 tomatoes (quartered)
2 quarts water	

1. In a large pot, place chuck, pork, salt, pepper and seasonings in 2 quarts water. Bring to a boil, then cover and simmer 1½ hours. Skim fat from surface with spoon.
2. With slicing disc in place, pack feed tube with carrots and process.
3. Next, pack feed tube with rutabaga and process.
4. Then in same manner process onions, followed by celery, potatoes and cabbage. Empty work bowl if it gets too full.
5. Add carrots, rutabaga, onions and cabbage to soup pot and bring to a boil. Cook 20 minutes.
6. Add celery and potatoes and cook 15 minutes.
7. Add tomatoes. Cook an additional 5 minutes and serve.

YIELD: *6–8 servings*

Jamaican Pepper Pot

My friend Jimmy Glenn's favorite vegetable is okra, and through him I came to discover the many things one can do with this delectable vegetable. This next one, indigenous to Jamaica, combines the flavors of cabbage, leeks, Tabasco and okra for a hearty soup that's sure to please.

Ingredients:

1½ pounds boned chuck (cut in 1-inch cubes)
3 cups water
1 tablespoon salt
½ teaspoon pepper
1 bay leaf
A few dashes of Tabasco
1 potato (peeled)
1 onion (peeled)

1 leek
1 can plum tomatoes (drained)
1 pound cabbage (cut in wedges)
1 green pepper (quartered)
1 bunch parsley
1 tablespoon flour
¾ pound fresh okra or 10-ounce package frozen

1. In large pot, place chuck, 3 cups water, salt, pepper, bay leaf and Tabasco. Bring to a boil, then cover and simmer 1½ hours.
2. Meanwhile, with slicing disc in place, pack the feed tube with potato. Process.
3. Next pack the onion in the feed tube and process.
4. Then pack and process the leek, followed by the tomatoes.
5. Empty the work bowl and pack the cabbage wedges into the feed tube. Repeat until all of it is processed.
6. Add all the vegetables to the soup pot and cook covered for 20 minutes.
7. Switch to steel blade. Add pepper and parsley to work bowl and process until finely minced. Add to soup pot.
8. Take ¼ cup of the broth out of the soup pot and blend in a small bowl with flour until smooth.
9. Stir mixture back into the soup pot along with the okra.
10. Cook covered 10 more minutes or until meat and vegetables are tender. Serve.

YIELD: *4–6 servings*

Zucchini Lamb Bake

Ingredients:

½ bunch parsley (rinsed, dried and stems removed)
1 clove garlic (peeled)
3 onions (peeled and quartered)
1 pound boneless lamb shoulder (cut into pieces)
1 pound zucchini (ends trimmed)

4 tablespoons butter
⅛ teaspoon pepper
1 teaspoon salt
½ teaspoon cinnamon
¼ teaspoon nutmeg
1 cup water
8 eggs

TOMATO SAUCE:

½ bunch parsley (rinsed, dried and stems removed)
1 clove garlic (peeled)
1 28-ounce can Italian plum tomatoes

1 small can tomato paste
½ teaspoon oregano
½ teaspoon basil
¼ teaspoon salt
⅛ cup red wine (optional)

1. Preheat oven to 375°. With steel blade in place, add parsley to work bowl. With motor running, drop garlic through feed tube. Process until finely minced.
2. Stop machine. Remove cover and add onions to work bowl. Process until coarsely chopped. Empty work bowl into large bowl and set aside.
3. With steel blade in place, add lamb to work bowl and process until well ground. Empty work bowl into bowl with onions. Set aside.
4. Switch to slicing disc. Pack feed tube with zucchini and process until all zucchini is sliced. Set aside.
5. Sauté lamb and onion mixture in butter in large frying pan until meat is browned.
6. Add zucchini, seasonings and water. Cook over low heat, stirring occasionally until meat and vegetables are tender. Then turn off heat and let cool.
7. With electric mixer, beat eggs until frothy.
8. Stir into meat mixture.
9. Pour into 1 quart baking dish and bake at 375° for 30 minutes or until set. Serve hot with sauce.

Tomato Sauce:

1. With steel blade in place, add parsley to work bowl. With motor running, drop garlic through feed tube and process until finely minced.
2. Stop machine. Remove cover and add tomatoes, paste, oregano, basil, salt and wine. Process until combined.
3. Pour into large saucepan and heat gently until needed.

YIELD: *4–6 servings*

Momma's Meatloaf

Another simple treat from Momma Viscardi that has that special touch. Italians thrive on tomato sauce, and meatloaf in our house was not acceptable without it!

Ingredients:

1 small bunch parsley (rinsed, dried and stems removed; reserve half for garnish)
1 clove garlic (peeled)
1 pound chuck or round ground beef

1 slice bread without crust (broken into pieces)
1 egg beaten
1 tablespoon grated Parmesan cheese
½ teaspoon salt
⅛ teaspoon pepper

SAUCE:
1 8-ounce can tomato sauce (or 1 cup homemade)

½ teaspoon oregano
½ cup water

1. With steel blade in place, add ½ bunch parsley to work bowl. Process until coarsely chopped, adding garlic with motor running until minced. Stop machine.
2. Add meat, bread, egg, cheese, salt and pepper. Process until combined.
3. Shape mixture into loaf, place in baking pan and brown in 350° oven for 20 minutes.
4. Remove from oven. Pour sauce over loaf. Add water to sauce can or measuring cup. Add oregano and pour over meat. Return to oven and bake 1 hour.
5. Garnish with rest of parsley and serve.

YIELD: *4–6 servings*

Stuffed Cabbage in Tomato Sauce

Ingredients:

Water for cooking
12 large cabbage leaves
1 large onion (peeled and quartered)
1 carrot (scrubbed and cut in 2-inch pieces)
½ bunch parsley (rinsed, dried and stems removed)
1 clove garlic (peeled)

6 tablespoons butter
1 pound ground round
½ pound ground pork
1 cup cooked brown rice
1 egg (lightly beaten)
1 teaspoon salt, or to taste
⅛ teaspoon pepper
½ teaspoon basil

SAUCE:
½ bunch parsley (rinsed, dried and stems removed)
1 clove garlic (peeled)
1 bunch fresh dill (rinsed, dried and stems removed)
2 tablespoons flour

1 cup tomato juice
½ cup water
½ pint sour cream
½ teaspoon salt
⅛ teaspoon pepper
¼ teaspoon oregano

1. Fill a large pot ¾-full with water and bring to boil. Blanch cabbage leaves by plunging in boiling water for 5 minutes. Drain well and set aside.
2. With steel blade in place, add onion, carrot, parsley and garlic to work bowl. Process until coarsely chopped.
3. Heat 2 tablespoons butter in large frying pan. Add onion mixture and sauté 3–5 minutes. Remove to large bowl.
4. Add meats and rice to bowl and mix well.
5. Add egg, salt, pepper and basil and mix again.
6. On work surface, flatten cabbage leaves. Place portion of meat mixture on each leaf and roll up leaves, tucking in ends to seal. They can be secured with toothpicks or string.
7. Heat the remaining 4 tablespoons of butter in the same large frying pan and gently sauté the cabbage rolls until lightly browned (4–5 minutes).
8. Reduce heat to low, cover pan and cook for 30 minutes.
9. Meanwhile, with steel blade in place, begin sauce by adding parsley, garlic and dill to work bowl and process until finely minced. Set aside.
10. Remove cabbage rolls to platter and discard toothpicks or string. Place in warm oven to keep hot.
11. Add the flour to frying pan, stirring constantly for 2 minutes.
12. Stir in tomato juice and water and bring to boil.
13. Blend in sour cream and dill and garlic mixture. Season with salt, pepper and oregano. Stir until heated through, about 1 minute.
14. Pour sauce over cabbage rolls and serve.

YIELD: *6 servings*

Ada Chiofalo's Target Meatloaves

The Chiofalo family have been delighting Baltimoreans with their homemade Italian food for years. Their restaurant is known for great food that only gets better as the years go by. Ada has generously contributed many of their recipes to my books, so now you can enjoy their great food even if you can't get to Baltimore!

These little gems are right on target for sure! Each person is served with their own little meatloaf, topped with a light tomato sauce.

Ingredients:

6 Saltines
1 small stalk celery (cut into 1-inch lengths)
½ bunch parsley (rinsed, dried and stems removed)
½ onion (peeled and quartered)
1 clove garlic (peeled)

1 egg
¼ cup milk
½ teaspoon salt
1 teaspoon oregano
1 pound ground beef
6 hard boiled eggs
1 teaspoon oil

SAUCE:

½ bunch parsley (rinsed, dried and stems removed)
½ onion (peeled and quartered)
1 8-ounce can tomato sauce

¼ cup water
½ teaspoon basil
½ teaspoon salt
½ teaspoon pepper

1. With steel blade in place, add Saltines to work bowl and process to make coarse crumbs. Remove and set aside.
2. With steel blade in place, add celery, parsley and onion to work bowl. Cover and start processor. Immediately drop garlic down feed tube and process 3 seconds or until finely chopped.
3. To onion mixture in work bowl, add egg, milk, salt, oregano and ground beef. Process briefly until well combined. Add Saltine crumbs and process briefly to combine.
4. Remove mixture from work bowl. Divide into 6 equal portions. Wrap each portion around a hard boiled egg. Place in single layer in an 8 x 12-inch baking dish greased with oil. Preheat oven to 350°.
5. Prepare sauce. In clean work bowl fitted with steel blade, process parsley and onion until finely minced.
6. Add remaining sauce ingredients to minced parsley and onion in work bowl. Cover and process briefly until well combined. Pour sauce over loaves in baking dish.
7. Bake in 350° oven for 1 hour, basting loaves several times with the sauce.

YIELD: *6 servings*

Poached Chicken Breasts with Chestnut Sauce

Ingredients:

½ pound chestnuts
Boiling water for cooking
unpeeled chestnuts
1 stalk celery (cut in 2-inch
lengths)
¾ cup milk plus ¾ cup water
1 bay leaf
½ teaspoon dried thyme
2 large boneless whole chicken
breasts

1 cup water
1 cup white wine
1 clove garlic
1 onion (peeled and quartered)
1 carrot (quartered)
2 tablespoons butter
3 tablespoons cream
¼ teaspoon nutmeg
Salt
Pepper

1. To peel chestnuts, drop into boiling water for 8 minutes. Turn the heat off, and while still hot, remove a few at a time and peel. Set aside.
2. With steel blade in place, add celery to work bowl and process until coarsely chopped.
3. Place chestnuts in pot. Cover with milk and water mixture.
4. Add celery, bay leaf and thyme. Simmer over low heat for 1 hour.
5. Meanwhile, prepare chicken for poaching by placing in deep skillet with water, wine, garlic, onion and carrot. Cover, bring to a boil and simmer 12 minutes.
6. When chestnuts are done, remove bay leaf, drain liquid and reserve. Add chestnuts to work bowl with steel blade in place. Process until smooth. Add butter, nutmeg, cream and salt and pepper to taste to work bowl. Process just until combined. Pour in a bit of reserved liquid through feed tube until desired consistency is reached. It should be the consistency of thick mayonnaise.
7. Pour purée over hot chicken breasts and serve.

YIELD: *2–4 servings*

Leonard's Favorite: Perfect Chicken Fried Rice

For most of my life I have been an actress. For years I did a lot of Off-Broadway shows and some TV commercials but I finally tired of audition lines and "go-see's" and began to explore different career paths. Writing and food were my great loves and almost before I knew it, they came together and my life as a cookbook writer had begun. Then a funny thing happened. After my first book, *Getting into Your Wok with Annette Anne-child,* came out, I was asked to do a television guest appearance for publicity. After it was over, everyone was amazed at how comfortable I was on camera and how well the segment went. I was soon asked to do more and more television and before long it became clear that my career as an actress was integral to my career as a food personality. Funny how life is . . . when the possibility for my own TV show surfaced, I quickly called the man who was the best director I had ever known as an actress—Leonard Peters. He became my acting coach once again—now with food as the focal point of my theatrics.

Well, aside from being an expert on acting, Leonard is known for his expertise on fried rice. It's his favorite dish and he orders it everywhere. I consulted with him on this one and he assures me that what we came up with is indeed perfect!

Ingredients:

6 mushrooms	Oil for cooking
2 carrots (scrubbed and cut to fit feed tube)	1 teaspoon sesame seeds
	¼ cup bean sprouts
2 scallions (ends trimmed and cut to fit feed tube)	4 cups cold cooked brown rice
	3 tablespoons tamari, or to taste
1 whole boneless breast of chicken (partially frozen)	2 eggs (beaten)

1. With slicing disc in place, pack feed tube with mushrooms in horizontal position. Process with moderate pressure on food pusher until all are sliced. Remove and set aside.
2. Process carrots with slicing disc, packing feed tube with them in vertical position and using light pressure on food pusher. Empty work bowl. Set aside.
3. Process scallions with slicing disc and firm pressure on food pusher, packing feed tube with them in vertical position. Remove and set aside.
4. Pack feed tube with partially frozen chicken and process with slicing disc using firm pressure on food pusher.
5. Heat about 3 tablespoons oil in wok or large skillet. Add chicken pieces and sesame seeds. Stir fry until chicken is white. Remove and set aside.
6. Add more oil if necessary and add carrots to wok or skillet. Stir fry until crisp-tender.
7. Add mushrooms and scallions. Stir fry 1 minute and add chicken back in, stirring to combine.

8. Add more oil if necessary and add sprouts and rice. Stir constantly.
9. Add tamari. Stir.
10. Make well in center of rice and add beaten eggs to well.
11. Stir to coat rice for 2 minutes and serve.

YIELD: *2 servings*

Game Hens with Cranberry Chestnut Stuffing

Ingredients:

2 cups chestnuts (peeled)
1 large stalk celery (trimmed and cut in 1-inch pieces)
1 pound fresh cranberries (picked over and rinsed)
1 cup whole wheat or cornbread crumbs
1 teaspoon sage
½ teaspoon marjoram
1 teaspoon freshly ground pepper
½ teaspoon salt
½ cup chicken broth
4 game hens (about 1½ pounds each)
4 tablespoons unsalted butter
Salt and freshly ground pepper to taste
½ cup dry red wine
2 ripe peaches (peeled, pitted and quartered)
½ cup water
¼ cup fresh mint leaves

1. Preheat oven to 350°. Simmer chestnuts in boiling water to cover for 10 minutes. Drain well and cool slightly.
2. With steel blade in place, add celery to work bowl. Process with several on/off bursts until coarsely chopped.
3. Add chestnuts and half of the cranberries to work bowl. Process 8–10 on/off bursts until mixture is coarsely chopped.
4. Add bread crumbs, sage, marjoram, 1 teaspoon pepper and ½ teaspoon salt to cranberry mixture in work bowl. Drizzle chicken broth over mixture. Process briefly just to combine.
5. Stuff game hens with the cranberry mixture. Skewer neck openings to keep stuffing enclosed. Rub each hen with 1 tablespoon of the butter and sprinkle with salt and pepper to taste.
6. Place hens on a rack in a shallow roasting pan. Roast in 350° oven for 15 minutes. Pour dry red wine over birds and continue roasting for another 45 minutes. Baste every 10 minutes with pan juices.
7. While hens are roasting, combine remaining cranberries, peaches, water and mint in saucepan. Bring to the boil and simmer about 10 minutes until cranberries pop open.
8. With steel blade in place, add cranberry and peach mixture to work bowl and purée. Return to saucepan and keep warm.
9. When hens are done, remove from oven and let rest 10 minutes. Remove skewers and serve with cranberry peach sauce.

YIELD: *4 servings*

Stir Fried Cashew Chicken in Oyster Sauce

Oyster sauce is a wonderful condiment to discover. It's available bottled in most grocery stores and all Oriental markets. The flavor is terrific!

Ingredients:

1 carrot (scrubbed and cut to fit feed tube)
1 zucchini (ends removed and cut to fit feed tube)
1 onion (peeled)
1 pound boneless breast of chicken (partially frozen and skin removed)
Oil for cooking

½ cup raw cashews
½ pound fresh snowpeas or 1 package frozen (ends clipped if fresh)
2 tablespoons water
¼ cup oyster sauce
2 cups hot cooked brown rice (see page 117)

1. With slicing disc in place, pack feed tube with carrots and process until sliced.
2. Process the zucchini the same way. Then empty work bowl. Set aside.
3. With slicing disc in place, pack feed tube with onion and process. Empty work bowl. Set aside separately.
4. With slicing disc in place, pack feed tube with partially frozen chicken and process. Set aside separately.
5. Heat wok or large skillet and necklace with oil.
6. Add chicken and cashews and stir fry until chicken is white and cashews golden. Remove to plate.
7. Add carrot, zucchini and onion and stir fry, adding more oil if necessary.
8. When onion is translucent and vegetables crisp-tender, add the snowpeas and chicken and cashews back to the wok.
9. Add water and oyster sauce and stir to combine. Cook 2–3 minutes more to heat through and serve with rice.

YIELD: *2 servings*

Chapter **7**

SIDE DISHES

Broccoli and Cauliflower Swirl

Ingredients:

½ head cauliflower (broken into pieces)
1 bunch broccoli (flowerets separated and stems trimmed)
¼ pound Gruyère cheese
½ teaspoon salt
½ teaspoon white pepper
1 large scallion (trimmed and cut in 1-inch pieces)
2 large eggs (separated)
Juice of 1 lemon
1 tablespoon butter

1. Steam cauliflower pieces until tender, about 10 minutes.
2. While cauliflower is steaming, prepare broccoli. With slicing disc in place, load feed tube with broccoli stems and process with firm pressure on feed tube for thick slices. Remove from work bowl and set aside.
3. Switch to shredding disc and shred Gruyère. Remove to small bowl and set aside.
4. When cauliflower is tender, rinse under cold water to stop cooking. Drain well.
5. Place broccoli flowerets and sliced stems in steamer, keeping them in separate piles if possible. Steam until tender, about 7 minutes.
6. While broccoli is steaming, insert steel blade in work bowl and add cauliflower. Process until puréed. Stop processor and add shredded Gruyère, salt and white pepper. Process briefly to combine. Remove to 1-quart bowl and set aside. Preheat oven to 375°.
7. When broccoli is tender, rinse with cold water and drain well. Reserve flowerets. With steel blade in place, add broccoli stems and scallion to work bowl. Process until puréed. Stop processor. Add egg yolks—place whites in 1-quart bowl—and lemon juice. Process until well combined.
8. Remove broccoli purée to 2-quart bowl. Stir in reserved flowerets.
9. Beat egg whites with hand mixer or whisk until they hold stiff peaks. Fold quickly but thoroughly into cauliflower and cheese mixture.
10. Fold cauliflower mixture into broccoli just to combine. The effect should be marbleized—green and white.
11. Pour mixture into 1½-quart buttered casserole or soufflé dish. Bake at 375° 20 minutes or until puffed and just beginning to brown. Serve immediately.

YIELD: *4–6 servings*

Brown Rice Pilaf

Ingredients:

1 medium onion (peeled and quartered)
1 large carrot (scraped and cut in 2-inch pieces)
2 tablespoons oil
2⅓ cups brown rice
4 cups boiling water
1 tablespoon tamari

1. With steel blade in place, add onion and carrot to work bowl. Process until finely chopped.
2. Heat oil in 2-quart heavy-bottomed saucepan. Add minced vegetables and sauté, stirring for 2 minutes.
3. Add rice and sauté, stirring for several minutes.
4. Add boiling water and tamari. Cover and simmer 45 minutes. Remove from heat, fluff with fork, recover and let stand 15 minutes.

YIELD: *4–6 servings*

Cold Noodles Szechuan Style

If you are a fan of Chinese restaurants, you undoubtedly have discovered the wonders of Cold Noodles Szechuan Style. They are also known as Cold Noodles with Sesame Sauce or Hot Peanut Noodles. Whatever they are called, they're great. They are also one of the most addictive foods I've ever tasted. I tried for years to get the recipe from my favorite Chinese restaurants, but to no avail. If they *did* give me a recipe, it never worked out when I rushed home to test it. Recipes published in other books also never duplicated the spectacular flavor.

So I decided to hold a little contest. I told all my fellow food people that whoever came up with the perfect recipe for this dish would be published with full credit in whatever book was under way at the time. Well, I must say that over the years we all came up with some wonderful dishes. Russell Bennett brought his Tahini Noodles. It was very good, but not perfect. Barbara Tint came very close but somehow it just wasn't *exactly* right. Well, I'm proud to announce we now have a winner! Skip Skwarek of "EATS!" did it! Here we have it, the perfect blend of the perfect ingredients! Now we can all finally have those great noodles at home. Bravo, Skip!

Ingredients:

2 large scallions (trimmed and cut in 1-inch pieces)
1 2-inch piece fresh ginger root (peeled and cut in half)
3 large cloves garlic (peeled)
3 tablespoons Toasted Almond Butter (see page 64)
3 tablespoons sesame oil
3 tablespoons tamari
3 tablespoons rice wine vinegar
2 tablespoons dry sherry
2 tablespoons honey
1 tablespoon hot chili oil
1 pound Japanese soba noodles or linguine

1. With steel blade in place, add scallions to work bowl. Cover and start processor. Immediately drop ginger pieces and garlic down feed tube. Process until finely minced.
2. Add remaining sauce ingredients to work bowl. Process briefly until well combined. Remove to small bowl and set aside.
3. Cook noodles according to package directions. Drain and rinse with cool water.
4. Place noodles in large serving bowl. Pour half of sauce over noodles and toss to coat.
5. Top each serving with about 1 tablespoon of the reserved sauce. Very spicy, very delicious and great served hot or cold.

YIELD: *4 servings (or about 1 cup of sauce)*

NOTE: For another way to use this sauce, see Grilled Sea Bass with Endive (page 81).

From Russell Bennett's Kitchen:

Imambaldi

This Middle Eastern dish has a legend to go along with its exotic flavor. Legend has it that a sultan invited a priest to dinner but neglected to tell his wife. She scurried into the kitchen on his arrival and blended all her leftovers together to create a dish the priest loved. They drank and ate for hours and to their surprise, the priest fainted! Hence the name "Imambaldi" which translates to "the priest has fainted." On his revival, he sputtered that the reason he had fainted was that he was overwhelmed with how wonderful her dinner had been!

Ingredients:

½ bunch fresh parsley (rinsed, dried and stems removed)
1 large onion (peeled and quartered)
1 clove garlic (peeled)
1 cup brine-cured black olives (pitted)

2 large eggplants
1 large or 2 small tomatoes (quartered)
1½ cups olive oil
¾ cup currants
1 tablespoon fresh curry powder
⅛ teaspoon ground pepper

1. With steel blade in place, add parsley to work bowl. Process until chopped finely. Remove and set aside.
2. With steel blade in place, add onion to work bowl. Process, and with motor running, add garlic through feed tube. Process until onion is coarsely chopped. Remove and set aside.
3. With steel blade in place, add olives to work bowl and process until finely chopped. Remove and set aside.
4. Cut eggplant into 2-inch thick rounds (about 3 rounds to an eggplant).
5. Scoop out eggplant pulp leaving a ⅔-inch thick cup-like shell.
6. With steel blade in place, add eggplant pulp to work bowl and process until finely chopped. Remove and set aside.
7. With steel blade in place, add tomatoes to work bowl and process until coarsely chopped.
8. Heat ½ cup olive oil in large skillet and sauté onions covered over low heat for 5 minutes, stirring occasionally.
9. Add all other ingredients except remaining olive oil and eggplant cups.
10. Sauté 3 minutes. Turn off heat.
11. Place 1 cup olive oil in baking pan. Add eggplant cups. With your fingers, rub all over the eggplant with oil. Have all cups face up.
12. Fill cups with mixture. Cover with aluminum foil.
13. Bake in preheated 375° oven 30 minutes covered, 15 minutes uncovered. Take out. Let cool, pouring off excess oil. Serve. Traditionally served cold, but it's wonderful warm, too!

YIELD: *4–6 servings*

From Russell Bennett's Kitchen:

Artichokes with Lemon Mustard Dip

Ingredients:

4 artichokes
Juice of 1 lemon plus juice of ½ lemon
1 clove garlic (peeled)
1 egg at room temperature
1 tablespoon rice vinegar

⅛ teaspoon cayenne pepper
½ teaspoon honey or sugar
¼ cup coarse mustard
¾ cup peanut oil
2 quarts water with ½ cup lemon juice added

1. Cut bottoms of artichokes off so that they will stand upright. Also slice about 1 inch off tops and de-barb by trimming sharp ends of petals off with scissors. Quickly rub bottoms and tops with juice of ½ lemon. Set aside.
2. With steel blade in place, turn machine on and drop garlic through feed tube until minced.
3. Remove cover. Add egg, rice vinegar, cayenne pepper, honey and mustard to work bowl. Process, and with motor running, slowly pour in oil and juice of whole lemon through feed tube.
4. Process until creamy. Refrigerate.
5. In large pot, place water and lemon juice mixture and bring to boil.
6. Place artichokes face down. Top artichokes with flat plate to hold them down. Cover and cook 20 minutes over medium heat.
7. Test after 20 minutes by piercing bottom with fork. Cook longer if necessary, until tender.
8. When done, drain by placing face down in baking pan until they reach room temperature.
9. Flip over and de-barb by removing furry choke from center of artichokes.
10. When ready to serve, fill center of artichokes with dip and enjoy.

YIELD: *4 servings*

From Russell Bennett's Kitchen:

Sautéed Brussels Sprouts with Ellison's Tweed Sauce

Fresh Brussels sprouts are a true joy to behold. They grow on a cone-shaped stalk, giving the appearance of tiny Christmas trees. In this recipe, they are steamed and topped with an alfalfa sprout-based sauce and seasoned with nutmeg. The sauce is unusual because instead of using eggs, cheese or milk to give it body (and calories!), we used alfalfa sprouts. It really worked well and now, for fewer calories and lots of vitamin C you can purée sprouts in your food processor as a base for many sauces. We named the sauce "Ellison's Tweed Sauce" at the suggestion of New York gourmet Ellison Billias, a friend who dropped in at the perfect moment to join us for a taste-testing meal!

Ingredients:

1 pint fresh Brussels sprouts (rinsed and tough bottoms trimmed)	1 cup alfalfa sprouts (packed tightly)
	3–4 tablespoons peanut oil
2 small onions or 1 medium onion (peeled)	1 teaspoon tamari
	1 teaspoon lemon juice
2 tablespoons butter	⅛ teaspoon nutmeg

1. Place Brussels sprouts in steam rack, covered, over boiling water in saucepan. Steam until tender, about 5 minutes. Turn off heat.
2. With steel blade in place, add onions to work bowl. Process until coarsely chopped.
3. Heat butter in skillet. Sauté onion until transparent. Turn off heat.
4. With steel blade in place, add alfalfa sprouts to work bowl. Process, pouring oil through feed tube. Turn off machine and scrape down sides.
5. Add tamari and lemon juice through feed tube. Process until smooth.
6. Add sauce to onions, season with nutmeg and sauté over very low heat until warmed.
7. Resteam Brussels sprouts for 1 minute if needed to heat.
8. Toss hot Brussels sprouts with warm sauce in skillet and serve.

YIELD: *4 servings*

Carrot Purée with Yogurt

Ingredients:

½ cup walnuts
1 pound carrots (scrubbed well)
1 large scallion (cut in 1-inch pieces)
1 1-inch piece fresh ginger (peeled)

1 tablespoon unsalted butter
¼ teaspoon ground coriander
2 tablespoons lemon juice
½ cup plain yogurt

1. Preheat oven to 350°. Spread walnuts in single layer and toast in oven 5 minutes.
2. Add toasted nuts to work bowl fitted with steel blade and process for 3 1-second bursts or until coarsely chopped. Remove to bowl and set aside.
3. Remove steel blade and insert slicing disc. Pack feed tube with carrots vertically. Process using light pressure on feed tube for thin slices.
4. In large saucepan bring 1 quart water to boil over high heat. Add sliced carrots and cook about 2 minutes until carrots are tender but not mushy. Drain and rinse with cold water to stop cooking. Set aside.
5. Add scallion pieces to work bowl fitted with steel blade. Cover and start processor. Immediately drop ginger through feed tube and process 3 seconds or until finely chopped.
6. In 1-quart heavy-bottomed saucepan, melt butter over medium heat. Add chopped scallions, ginger and coriander. Sauté, stirring, for 1 minute. Remove from heat and add drained carrots and lemon juice. Combine well.
7. With steel blade in place, purée the mixture (in batches if your work bowl is not large). Return the purée to 1-quart saucepan. Add yogurt and combine well. Place over low heat and stir until heated through.
8. Serve garnished with toasted chopped walnuts.

YIELD: *4 servings*

Zesty Rutabaga Salad

Ingredients:

1 bunch parsley (rinsed, dried and stems removed)

1 pound rutabaga (peeled and quartered)

2 large carrots (scrubbed and cut in 2-inch lengths)

½ cup orange juice

Salt and pepper to taste

1. With steel blade in place, add parsley to work bowl and process until coarsely chopped. Stop machine.
2. Add rutabaga and carrots to work bowl and process until coarsely chopped, then stop machine.
3. Pour orange juice in through feed tube. Process 1–2 seconds, just to combine. Remove to bowl, add salt and pepper to taste and mix well.
4. Refrigerate until ready to serve.

YIELD: *4 servings*

Carrot Nests

Ingredients:

½ cup raisins
½ cup orange juice
1 pound carrots (scrubbed well)
4 tablespoons unsalted butter
2 teaspoons cumin seeds

1 tablespoon fresh ginger (peeled and shredded)
2 cloves garlic (minced)
1 tablespoon lemon juice
¼ teaspoon freshly ground pepper
Salt to taste

1. In small saucepan, simmer raisins in orange juice until plump, about 10 minutes.
2. While raisins are simmering, shred carrots in processor fitted with shredding disc.
3. In large saucepan, bring to boil 1 quart water over high heat. Add shredded carrots and stir for 1 minute. Drain in fine sieve and rinse with cold water to stop cooking. Set aside.
4. In frying pan or wok, melt 1 tablespoon butter over medium heat. Add cumin seeds and sauté 30 seconds. Add ginger and garlic. Sauté 1 minute.
5. Add remaining 3 tablespoons butter. When melted and bubbling, add drained shredded carrots. Toss thoroughly to coat with butter and spices until heated through.
6. Sprinkle with lemon juice, pepper and salt to taste.
7. Arrange in mounds on 4 plates. Make well in center of each mound with back of spoon to form nest shape. Place heaping tablespoon drained plumped raisins in each nest.

YIELD: *4 servings*

Cottage Cheese Loaf

Ingredients:

4 slices stale whole wheat bread
1 scallion (trimmed and cut in 1-inch pieces)
1 carrot (peeled and cut in 1-inch pieces)
1 stalk celery (trimmed and cut in 1-inch pieces)
2 cups lima beans
1½ pounds cottage cheese
1 7-ounce jar roasted red peppers (drained)
1 teaspoon salt
⅛ teaspoon pepper
1 tablespoon butter for greasing pan
2 cups tomato sauce

1. Preheat oven to 350°.
2. Insert steel blade, break stale bread into pieces and process until crumbs are fine. Remove to 2-quart bowl.
3. With steel blade, process scallion, carrot and celery until finely chopped. Add to bowl with crumbs.
4. With steel blade, purée lima beans, cottage cheese, red peppers, salt and pepper until smooth. Add to bowl with crumb mixture and combine well.
5. Grease a 6-cup loaf pan with the butter and fill with cottage cheese mixture.
6. Bake in 350° oven for 30 minutes.
7. Meanwhile, heat tomato sauce in small saucepan. After loaf has baked for 30 minutes, pour 1 cup of the tomato sauce over it and bake 15 minutes longer.
8. Slice and serve with extra sauce.

YIELD: *1 loaf (6 servings)*

Cashew Celery Loaf

Ingredients:

½ cup toasted cashews
1 medium onion (peeled and quartered)
2 stalks celery (trimmed and cut in 1-inch pieces)
½ bunch parsley (stems removed)
2 hot green peppers (cored and seeded)
1 large egg
¾ cup tomato purée or juice

1 cup whole wheat bread crumbs
½ cup freshly grated Parmesan
1 teaspoon dried basil (or 2 tablespoons fresh)
1 teaspoon sage leaves (crumbled)
½ teaspoon salt
1 teaspoon oil
12 cashew halves for garnish

1. Preheat oven to 350°. Add cashews to work bowl fitted with steel blade and process 5–6 1-second bursts until coarsely chopped. Remove from bowl and set aside.
2. Replace work bowl and steel blade. Add onion, celery, parsley and green peppers. Cover and process 5–7 seconds or until finely chopped.
3. Remove cover. Add remaining ingredients except oil and cashew halves. Replace cover and process for several 1-second bursts or until well combined.
4. Oil a 2-cup casserole or loaf pan and fill with celery mixture. Garnish top of loaf with cashew halves.
5. Bake at 350° for 30 minutes. Slice and serve.

YIELD: *4 servings*

Nutty Beet Loaf

Ingredients:

1 onion (peeled and quartered)
2 cloves garlic (peeled)
1 1-inch piece peeled ginger root
1 small bunch fresh parsley
  (rinsed, dried and stems
  removed; reserve a small
  amount for garnish)
1¼ cups whole wheat bread
  crumbs

3 large or 4 medium beets
  (scraped and quartered)
12 ounces walnuts
3 tablespoons oil
1 teaspoon salt
⅛ teaspoon pepper
2 eggs (beaten)
½ cup yogurt
Oil

SAUCE:

16 ounces tofu (2 very large or 4
  small cakes, crumbled)
2 medium beets (scraped and
  quartered)
1 tablespoon tamari

1 teaspoon dried basil
1 1-inch piece ginger
1 teaspoon Dijon mustard
1 teaspoon Worcestershire sauce
2 tablespoons fresh dill

1. With steel blade in place, put quartered onion in work bowl. Cover, turn on machine and with motor running add garlic and ginger by dropping in feed tube. Process until minced. Stop machine and remove to bowl. Set aside.
2. With steel blade in place, add parsley, crumbs, beets and walnuts to work bowl. Process until finely minced.
3. In wok or large skillet, sauté minced garlic and onion in oil until golden.
4. Add beet mixture and salt and pepper to skillet. Sauté 3 minutes. Remove from heat.
5. Mix in beaten eggs and yogurt.
6. Spoon into oiled loaf pan and bake at 350° for 30 minutes.
7. To prepare sauce, add all ingredients to work bowl and process with steel blade until creamy. Heat gently and serve with loaf. Garnish with parsley.

YIELD: *1 loaf, or 4–6 servings*

NOTE: Leftovers are great sliced cold on sandwiches or dipped in egg and fried in oil.

The Best Potato Salad You've Ever Tasted

Ingredients:

2 pounds boiled potatoes (peeled)

1 large cucumber (peeled, seeded and cut into 2-inch pieces)

1 small bunch dill (rinsed, dried and stems removed)

4 large scallions (ends removed and cut into 2-inch lengths)

4 stalks celery (cut into 1-inch lengths)

½ dozen hard boiled eggs

2 large tomatoes (quartered)

½–1 cup mayonnaise (depending on how creamy you like it)

¼ pound blue cheese

Salt and pepper to taste

MARINADE:

6 tablespoons oil

3 tablespoons wine vinegar

1 teaspoon prepared mustard

½ teaspoon oregano

½ teaspoon basil

1. With slicing disc in place, pack feed tube with cooked potatoes and process until sliced.
2. Combine marinade ingredients in bowl and top with sliced potatoes. Refrigerate while working on the rest of recipe.
3. With steel blade in place, add cucumbers, dill, scallions and celery to work bowl. Process until coarsely chopped. Remove to large serving bowl.
4. With steel blade in place, add hard boiled eggs to work bowl and process until coarsely chopped. Add to celery mixture.
5. With steel blade in place, add tomatoes to work bowl. Process only until coarsely chopped. Add to celery mixture.
6. With steel blade in place, add mayonnaise and blue cheese to work bowl. Process until combined.
7. Add potatoes and marinade to serving bowl and toss with other vegetables.
8. Pour mayonnaise mixture over all ingredients in serving bowl. Season with salt and pepper to taste. Toss to combine. Refrigerate until ready to serve.

YIELD: *4–6 servings*

Fresh Cabbage Salad

Low in cost and calories, easy to prepare, cabbage is packed with potassium. As a salad, it's a perfect accompaniment to a picnic or buffet.

Ingredients:

1 small firm red cabbage
1 small firm green cabbage
Salt
2 small green Italian sweet peppers
2 cloves garlic (peeled)

1 teaspoon honey
Pepper to taste
6 tablespoons olive oil
2 tablespoons lemon juice
1 tablespoon caraway seeds

1. Remove outer leaves and cut cabbages into chunks, discarding core.
2. With shredding disc, shred cabbage.
3. Place shredded cabbage in colander. Sprinkle all over with salt and toss well.
4. Place a dish or any weighted object on top to press cabbage. It will lose water and soften after ½ hour standing time.
5. Insert steel blade and process sweet peppers and garlic until minced.
6. Add honey and pepper to processor bowl.
7. Then with motor running, add oil and lemon juice through feed tube.
8. After cabbage is tender, place in large salad bowl.
9. Add dressing and caraway seeds. Toss well.
10. Refrigerate and serve chilled.

YIELD: *4–6 servings*

Honey Glazed Rutabaga Apple Delight

Ingredients:

1 medium rutabaga (peeled)
1 medium apple (cored and quartered)

2 tablespoons butter
¼ cup honey

1. Preheat oven to 375°. With slicing disc in place, pack feed tube with rutabaga and process.
2. Process apple the same way.
3. Empty work bowl ingredients into casserole dish.
4. Dot with butter and drizzle with honey.
5. Bake ½ hour at 375° and serve.

YIELD: *2 servings*

Momma's Perfect Turkey Stuffing

Ingredients:

1 bunch parsley (rinsed, dried and stems removed)
1 onion (peeled and quartered)
1 large stale loaf wheat or white bread (cut into cubes)
1 teaspoon salt
1 teaspoon pepper
1 teaspoon poultry stuffing seasoning
1 tablespoon thyme
2 tablespoons butter (broken into small pieces)
1 cup chicken broth

1. With steel blade in place, place parsley and quartered onion in work bowl and process until coarsely chopped.
2. Place cubed bread in large bowl, add chopped onion and parsley, salt, pepper, poultry seasoning, thyme, and butter bits. Mix.
3. Add broth a little at a time, mixing well.
4. Place in turkey cavity just before roasting. It also can be baked in a baking pan by itself.

YIELD: *enough for a 14-pound turkey*

Chapter 8

DESSERTS AND OTHER NATURAL GOODIES

Fresh Kiwi Sorbet

These beautiful little fruits can be used in a great variety of dishes, from main course through dessert. Here, they are puréed and frozen in a classic sorbet. It is a perfect dessert for a hot summer evening.

Ingredients:

2 ½-inch strips lemon zest
½ cup dry vermouth
⅓ cup sugar plus 1 teaspoon sugar

4 fresh kiwis (peeled and quartered)
1 tablespoon fresh lemon juice
4 pineapple slices

1. Coat lemon zest with 1 teaspoon sugar and break into bits.
2. With steel blade in place, add sugar-coated zest bits to work bowl and process in short bursts until minced—it takes about 3 minutes.
3. Place vermouth and ⅓ cup sugar in saucepan. Bring to low boil over medium heat, stirring to dissolve sugar, and boil 6 minutes to make syrup—it should be light amber in color.
4. Meanwhile, place kiwis and lemon juice in work bowl with grated peel. Process about 2 minutes or until smooth.
5. Cool the syrup, then add to the kiwi purée in work bowl. Process until well blended (about 4 3-second bursts).
6. Pour into baking pan and place in freezer for 1 hour or until frozen.
7. Place chunks of frozen sorbet in work bowl and, with steel blade in place, process until puréed. The sorbet will need to soften a bit before it will purée. The consistency should be very whipped and creamy when finished.
8. Spoon into the center of 4 pineapple slices. Serve immediately.

YIELD: *4 servings*

NOTE: For variation: Sorbet can be made with fresh cantaloupe or pineapple instead of kiwi.

Perfect Flan

This recipe has been in Cristina's family for many years and is a real treat to be able to include here. It truly is perfect.

Ingredients:

3 eggs
1 teaspoon vanilla extract
1 tablespoon Cognac or sherry
1 14-ounce can condensed milk

2¼ cups whole milk
¼ cup sugar
1 cinnamon stick (broken into pieces)

1. Preheat oven to 350°. Place eggs, vanilla and Cognac or sherry in bowl of food processor. With steel blade in place, process for 3 seconds, or until eggs are lemon colored and all ingredients are combined.
2. Add condensed milk to processor and process for 3 seconds.
3. Add whole milk and process for an additional 3 seconds.
4. In cast iron skillet over low heat, melt sugar and brown lightly. Pour into bottom of buttered 1½ quart mold. Pour custard mix over melted sugar. Top with pieces of cinnamon stick.
5. Place mold into shallow pan filled halfway with boiling water. Bake at 350° on center rack for 1 to 1½ hours, or until custard is set. Test doneness by inserting knife in center. Flan is done if the knife comes out clean.
6. Cool, unmold and refrigerate overnight before serving.

YIELD: *6–8 servings*

A NOTE ABOUT PIE CRUSTS

The following recipe for Orange-Crusted Mango and Kiwi Pie uses a "long" or flaky crust. This type of dough requires a minimum of 4 hours refrigeration before rolling out the crust. The results are worth the wait: a light, tender and flaky crust strong enough to keep the juiciest pie from leaking, tender enough to melt in your mouth. So plan ahead and make the dough a day in advance, or keep a supply in your freezer. Thaw frozen dough in the refrigerator overnight and remove ½ hour before rolling.

Orange-Crusted Mango and Kiwi Pie

CRUST:

2 cups chilled unbleached all purpose flour
Zest from ½ an orange (cut into strips)
1 tablespoon sugar
½ teaspoon salt
8 tablespoons lard or solid vegetable shortening (chilled)

4 tablespoons butter (chilled)
¼–½ cup freshly squeezed ice cold orange juice
½ cup flour for rolling dough
2 tablespoons melted unsalted butter

FILLING:

⅓ cup sugar
2 tablespoons cornstarch
1 teaspoon cinnamon
¼ teaspoon ground coriander
¼ teaspoon nutmeg
2 large mangoes (ripe but not

mushy; peeled and cut in chunks)
4 large kiwis (peeled)
2 tablespoons Grand Marnier or orange juice

1. Chill flour in refrigerator for 20 minutes. With steel blade in place, add orange zest, sugar and salt to work bowl. Process until finely minced.
2. Add chilled flour, lard and butter to minced zest in work bowl. Process 4–5 on/off bursts or until mixture is the size of grains of raw rice.
3. With processor running, slowly pour ice cold orange juice down feed tube. Process just until dough forms a ball around shaft. (If dough forms a ball before all of the juice is added, stop processor and do *not* add remaining juice.) Dough should be moist enough to hold together but should not feel sticky.
4. Wrap dough airtight in waxed paper and chill at least 4 hours, or overnight.
5. Remove dough from refrigerator ½ hour before rolling. Grease a 9-inch pie plate with some of the melted butter. Lightly dust work surface with flour for rolling. Divide dough into 2 equal portions. Shape each into a ball and dust lightly with flour. Flatten ball in center of work surface. Dust rolling pin with flour and roll dough into a 12-inch circle, working from center of dough out. Fold dough over rolling pin and carefully lift and place in greased pie plate. Roll second ball of dough into 10-inch circle. Place on flat plate. Refrigerate both crusts while you prepare filling.
6. Preheat oven to 425°. With steel blade in place, add sugar, cornstarch, cinnamon, coriander and nutmeg to work bowl. Process 5–6 on/off bursts to sift and combine. Remove to small bowl and set aside.
7. With slicing blade in place, load feed tube with mango chunks. Process with light pressure on food pusher until all mango is sliced. Place whole peeled kiwis vertically in feed tube and process as for mango.
8. Remove sliced fruit to large bowl. Sprinkle sugar mixture over fruit and toss gently to combine.

9. Remove bottom crust from refrigerator. Fill with fruit mixture. Sprinkle fruit with Grand Marnier or orange juice.
10. Remove top crust from refrigerator. Carefully lay crust over fruit filling. Fold up overhang from bottom crust and press to seal with top crust. Crimp edges decoratively with fingers or tines of a fork. Brush top crust and crimped edge with remaining melted butter. Prick top crust in several places with fork to allow steam to escape.
11. Place pie on foil-lined cookie sheet. Bake at 425° for 15 minutes. Reduce heat to 350° and bake 30–40 minutes longer or until crust is golden brown.
12. Serve warm or chilled.

YIELD: *1 9-inch double-crusted pie*

Grand Marnier Sweet Potato Pudding

Ingredients:

5 medium size sweet potatoes (baked until tender)	4 eggs (beaten)
1 tablespoon butter	3½ cups milk
2 tablespoons honey	½ cup Grand Marnier
½ teaspoon salt	2 tablespoons butter
½ teaspoon cinnamon	Whipped cream for topping (optional)

1. Preheat oven to 325°.
2. While potatoes are warm, split and scoop out pulp.
3. With steel blade in place, add pulp and all other ingredients to work bowl and process until well combined. Be sure not to over-process.
4. Pour into 2-quart buttered casserole dish or individual greased custard cups.
5. Bake 45 minutes or until custard sets. Great with whipped cream!

YIELD: *8 servings*

Walnut Raisin Carrot Ring

Ingredients:

1¼ cups unbleached white flour
½ teaspoon salt
1 teaspoon baking powder
1 teaspoon baking soda
2 carrots (scrubbed and cut into 2-inch lengths)
½ cup raisins
½ cup walnuts

¾ cup butter
½ cup brown sugar
1 egg
1 teaspoon lemon juice
1 tablespoon water
2 tablespoons shortening for greasing pan
1 6-cup mold

1. With steel blade in place, add flour, salt, baking powder and soda to work bowl. Process 4–5 1-second bursts to sift. Remove to bowl and set aside.
2. With shredding disc in place, pack feed tube tightly with carrots and process with moderate pressure on food pusher until all carrots are shredded. Remove from work bowl. Set aside.
3. Change to steel blade. Add raisins and nuts to work bowl and process until coarsely chopped. Stop machine, remove nuts and raisins and set aside.
4. With steel blade in place, add butter and brown sugar to work bowl and process until creamed together. Stop machine.
5. Add egg and flour mixture to work bowl. Be sure food pusher is in place. Process until blended. Stop machine.
6. Add lemon juice, water, carrots, nuts and raisins to work bowl and process just until combined. Stop machine.
7. Pour into greased 6-cup mold.
8. Bake in preheated 350° oven for 45–50 minutes or until a knife inserted in center comes out clean. Let cool 10 minutes. Run knife around edges. Invert on cooling rack to remove.

Great served warm!

YIELD: *6–8 servings*

For Raymond's Sweet Tooth—
Southern Peachy Pecan Squares

As my career branched out from books into television, how I looked became as important as what I knew. Suddenly there were decisions about image and style that no longer were merely personally important—now they involved my career as well. I knew I wanted to stick close to the natural side of beauty, but everybody that was hired to do my hair and make-up seemed to want to change me into the slick model persona that is standard in the world of television. Then I met Raymond Heremaia of Le Salon in Beverly Hills. Raymond understood. Instead of piling on the make-up and hair spray and turning me into a caricature of myself, he began teaching me how to work on being beautiful from the inside out.

Agreeing that diet and exercise are the key, he went on to teach me the art of facial massage, deep breathing and natural products. I've never looked better. After accompanying me to a taping on the Regis Philbin Show, we decided to make dinner for some friends to celebrate. Raymond admitted that dessert was his favorite part of every meal, so to suit his tastes especially, I created this one.

When peaches are in season in your area, be sure to try this one—it's great!

Ingredients:

½ cup butter
½ cup dark brown sugar
1 cup unbleached white flour plus
  2 tablespoons flour
1 cup pecans
1 pound ripe peaches (peeled,
  pitted and quartered)
2 eggs

1 teaspoon vanilla
¼ teaspoon salt
½ cup light brown sugar
½ cup shredded coconut (or piece
  of peeled fresh coconut)
Whipped cream topping
  (optional)

1. Preheat oven to 350°. With steel blade in place, add butter and dark brown sugar to work bowl. Process until creamed together. Stop machine.
2. Add 1 cup flour to work bowl and process until combined. Stop machine. Remove mixture and press into bottom of greased 8 x 8-inch baking pan to form crust. Bake in 350° oven for 20 minutes.
3. Meanwhile, with steel blade in place, add pecans to work bowl. Process until coarsely chopped. Stop machine, remove and set aside in large bowl. (If using fresh coconut, cut in 1-inch chunks and process with steel blade until coarsely grated. Remove to bowl with pecans and set aside.)
4. Add peaches to work bowl and process until coarsely chopped. Remove to small bowl and set aside.
5. Add eggs, vanilla and salt to work bowl and process until frothy. With machine running, add light brown sugar 1 tablespoon at a time through feed tube. Process until thick.

6. Toss coconut and pecans with 2 tablespoons flour. Add egg mixture and mix well.
7. When crust has finished baking, spread with chopped peaches.
8. Top with pecan and egg mixture. Spread evenly over peaches.
9. Bake 20 more minutes at 350°. Cool, cut into squares and serve. Of course, it's heavenly with whipped cream!

YIELD: *64 1-inch squares*

John and Annie's Tofu Pie

Annie Fox is a gifted food therapist and consultant who lectures extensively to doctors, nurses and dieticians about the correct preparation of wholesome foods. She and her husband John's recipe for Tofu Pie is the best I've ever found. If you haven't already been convinced about the incredible versatility of tofu, you will be after this recipe. Here the tofu is sweetened and prepared to create a pie that can satisfy your sweet tooth with the texture of cheesecake *without* the calories and *with* the high protein. You'll need to take a trip to your natural food store for this one but the results are very much worth the trip!

Ingredients:

CRUST:
1½ cups of your favorite granola
¼ cup apple cider

¼ teaspoon almond extract

TOFU FILLING:
⅓ cup water
2 tablespoons oil or 1 tablespoon tahini
2 teaspoons vanilla extract
⅓ cup maple syrup

½ teaspoon Cafix (coffee substitute), optional
1 pound tofu (crumbled)
Juice of 1 lemon
Pinch of salt

TOPPING:
¼ cup unsulphered dried apricots
1¾ cups apple cider
Dash of cinnamon

1 vanilla bean (split)
1 tablespoon kuzo (see note)

1. Preheat oven to 375°.
2. With steel blade in place, add granola to work bowl and process until it forms coarse crumbs.
3. Pour into bowl, add apple cider and almond extract and mix with fork until well blended and moist.
4. Press into the bottom and sides of 8½-inch round pan. Set aside and prepare filling.
5. With steel blade in place, add all filling ingredients to work bowl. Process until smooth and pour into prepared crust.
6. Bake at 375° until golden and slightly puffy. Allow to cool completely.
7. Meanwhile, prepare topping:
   Simmer apricots covered in ¾ cup apple cider with cinnamon and vanilla bean for 30 minutes. There should be very little liquid left. Allow to cool.
8. Remove vanilla bean.
9. With steel blade in place, add apricot mixture to clean work bowl with ½ cup more apple cider. Process until smooth.
10. Dissolve kuzo in remaining cider. Pour into saucepan.
11. Add apricot purée and simmer, stirring constantly until very thick and glossy.
12. Pour over top of cooled pie to form glaze and chill until it sets, then serve. It tastes great made a day in advance!

NOTE: Kuzo is available in natural food stores.   YIELD: *1 8½-inch pie*

Cinnamon Walnut Crescents

Ingredients:

½ cup butter
½ cup shortening
⅓ cup sugar
2 teaspoons ice water
2 teaspoons vanilla

2 cups flour
2 teaspoons cinnamon
½ cup chopped walnuts
Confectioners' sugar for dipping

1. With steel blade in place, add butter, shortening and sugar to work bowl and process until thoroughly creamed together.
2. To work bowl, add ice water and vanilla and process 4 seconds.
3. Add flour, cinnamon and walnuts to work bowl and process until mixed well.
4. Chill 3 or 4 hours.
5. Form dough into long rolls ½-inch in diameter.
6. Cut in 3-inch lengths and shape into crescents.
7. Bake on ungreased cookie sheet at 325° for 15 minutes. Do not brown.
8. Remove from sheet. Cool slightly and dip in confectioner's sugar.

YIELD: *4 dozen crescents*

Chocolate Cream Cheese Cookies

Ingredients:

¼ teaspoon salt
1¼ cups sifted unbleached white
    flour
½ cup butter
3 ounces cream cheese

½ cup grated or shredded
    coconut
½ cup sugar
1 teaspoon vanilla
1 egg yolk
1 cup chocolate bits

1. Sprinkle salt over flour and set aside.
2. With steel blade in place, add butter, cream cheese and coconut to work bowl. Process until creamed together. Stop machine.
3. Add sugar, vanilla and egg yolk to work bowl and process until light and fluffy. Stop machine.
4. Add flour and salt mixture to work bowl and process *only* until blended. Stop machine.
5. Add chocolate bits to work bowl and process very briefly, just until chocolate is mixed into batter.
6. Make 1-inch balls by hand with dough. Place on greased cookie sheet. Flatten balls slightly with bottom of glass.
7. Bake at 350° for 15 minutes.

YIELD: *3½ dozen cookies*

Steve's Favorite

Steve Eisenberg's real favorite is his wife Cristina, and with good reason. Aside from being smart, beautiful and kind, she's perfect in the kitchen. She makes food fun—letting her imagination and love lead the way. This recipe was a recent midnight snack she surprised him with during late night TV. What a wife!

Ingredients:

4 medium size tart apples
½ cup brown sugar plus ¼ cup brown sugar
¼ cup slivered almonds
¼ cup raisins
1 tablespoon dry sherry

1 teaspoon vanilla extract
1 egg white
½ cup fine bread crumbs
¼ teaspoon cinnamon
¼ teaspoon ginger
1 stick butter (melted)

1. Preheat oven to 350°.
2. Peel and core the apples. Place in a buttered 8 x 8-inch baking pan.
3. With steel blade in place, put ½ cup brown sugar, almonds, and raisins in bowl of processor. Process 3–5 seconds, or until well mixed. Add sherry, vanilla extract and egg white and process an additional 5 seconds. Set aside.
4. Place bread crumbs, cinnamon, ginger and ¼ cup brown sugar in bowl of food processor. With steel blade in place, process 5 seconds or until thoroughly blended. Place in shallow dish and set aside.
5. Brush apples with some of the melted butter. Stuff with almond and raisin mixture and roll in bread crumb mixture.
6. Drizzle remaining butter over top of apples. Bake at 350° for 45 minutes.
7. 15 minutes before apples are done, remove from oven and baste with pan juices. Return to oven and continue baking.
8. Serve hot or cold. For a truly sinful dessert, serve on a cloud of whipped cream, sprinkled with cinnamon.

YIELD: *4 servings*

Hot Apple Puffs

These are a great dessert to have on hand in the refrigerator. Then, almost instantly, you can create little hot apple pies for unexpected company!

Ingredients:

1 cup flour
Tiny pinch salt
1 teaspoon baking powder
3 tart apples (cored, peeled and quartered)
¼ teaspoon cinnamon

2 teaspoons coconut
¼ cup raisins
1 egg
1 cup milk
3 tablespoons sugar
3 cups oil for cooking

1. With steel blade in place, add flour, salt and baking powder to work bowl. Process with 5 short bursts to sift and combine. Remove and set aside.
2. With steel blade in place, add quartered apples to work bowl and process until coarsely chopped. Remove to bowl with flour.
3. Add cinnamon, coconut, raisins, egg, milk and sugar. Mix well. (At this stage, batter can be refrigerated until needed.)
4. Heat oil in wok or deep fryer.
5. Drop by the tablespoon into hot oil, a few at a time.
6. Drain on paper towels.
7. Serve hot or warm, with ice cream!

YIELD: *at least 12–15 puffs*

Almond Potato Cake

Ingredients:

⅔ cup toasted almonds
2 tablespoons unbleached all purpose flour
½ pound potatoes (boiled, peeled and chilled)
¼ pound unsalted butter at room temperature

¼ cup sugar
3 large eggs
1 tablespoon grated orange rind
½ teaspoon cinnamon
¼ teaspoon salt
Fresh whipped cream, ice cream, strawberries (optional)

1. Preheat oven to 350°.
2. Add almonds and flour to work bowl fitted with steel blade. Process until almonds are finely grated. Remove to 1-quart bowl and set aside.
3. Replace steel blade with shredding disc. Pack feed tube with chilled potatoes. Process with light pressure on food pusher for fine shreds. Repeat until all potatoes are shredded and add to ground almonds.
4. Replace shredding disc with plastic blade. Add butter and sugar to work bowl. Process until light and fluffy.
5. Separate eggs, adding yolks to creamed butter in work bowl and reserve whites in a 1-quart bowl. Add orange rind and cinnamon to work bowl. Process until well combined.
6. Add potatoes and almonds to mixture in work bowl. Process briefly just to combine. Remove to 2-quart bowl.
7. Add salt to egg whites and beat with electric mixer or whisk until they hold stiff peaks. Fold quickly but thoroughly into potato mixture.
8. Pour into buttered and floured 9-inch round cake pan. Smooth top with spatula and bake at 350° for 25–30 minutes or until cake is puffed and golden.
9. Serve warm plain or with any or all of the optional garnishes.

YIELD: *1 9-inch round cake*

Skip's Basic Egg Bread

It's great! Skip had his doubts about making bread with a food processor but now he's ecstatic about it! He's developed a very easy, fabulous tasting loaf that makes even a beginner a breadwinner!

Ingredients:

3 tablespoons honey plus 2 tablespoons honey for glaze
¼ cup peanut oil
1⅛ cups warm water, about 110° F.
3 ¼-ounce packages dry yeast

3½ cups unbleached white flour plus extra ½ cup flour
1. teaspoon salt
1 extra large egg (lightly beaten)
2 tablespoons butter (softened)

1. Combine 3 tablespoons honey, oil and warm water in 1-quart bowl. Add yeast and stir to dissolve. Set aside for 10–20 minutes (or until spongy-looking).
2. While yeast is proofing, place steel blade in work bowl and add 3½ cups flour and salt. Process with 5 1-second bursts to sift and combine.
3. When yeast mixture is ready, stir in all but 1 tablespoon of egg (save that for brushing top of loaf before baking).
4. Turn processor on. Pour yeast mixture through feed tube. As soon as all of yeast mixture is added, process 25 seconds or until the dough has pulled away from sides of work bowl and clings to center shaft. It will be *very* sticky.
5. Rub hands with some of the softened butter and lightly grease the inside of a large bowl. Scoop dough out of work bowl with buttered hands, form into ball and place in greased bowl. Cover loosely with plastic wrap. Set in a warm, draft-free place and let rise about 1 hour or until tripled in volume.
6. Punch down, re-cover and let rise again until tripled in volume.
7. After second rise, punch down and let dough rest 10 minutes.
8. Spread reserved ½ cup flour on work surface. Grease hands with remaining softened butter and lightly grease a 6-cup loaf pan. Divide dough into 3 equal portions. Dredge each portion lightly in flour on work surface. Knead slightly while shaping each portion into a ball.
9. Place the 3 balls of dough into the loaf pan, side by side so that all the balls are touching.
10. Brush reserved egg over top of dough.
11. Cover with plastic wrap and allow to rise for 20 minutes while oven is preheating to 350°.
12. Remove plastic wrap and bake at 350° for 40 minutes or until loaf is golden and sounds hollow when tapped.
13. Immediately turn loaf out of pan. Place on rack and brush top with 2 tablespoons honey. Cool completely.

YIELD: *1 loaf*

1 - 2 - 3 - 4 Cake

I don't know where this recipe originally came from but it's been in our family for years. I believe an old friend and neighbor, Jean Sanders, gave it to my mother long ago. It's been my birthday cake for many of the past 30 years. It has a rich, full flavor and now adapted for the food processor, it's easier to make than ever.

Ingredients:

3 cups flour
4 teaspoons baking powder
1 cup butter or margarine, or
  ½ cup of each

2 cups sugar
4 eggs
1 cup milk
2 teaspoons vanilla

1. With plastic blade in place, add flour and baking powder to work bowl. Process 4–5 1-second bursts to sift. Remove to bowl and set aside.
2. With plastic blade in place, add butter and sugar to work bowl. Process until creamed together. Stop machine.
3. Add eggs to work bowl. Process until combined. Stop machine.
4. Add half the flour mixture and half the milk to work bowl. Process until combined. Stop machine.
5. Add rest of flour mixture, milk and vanilla to work bowl and process until smooth.
6. Bake as loaf or layer cake in greased and floured pans. Bake 2 9-inch *layers* at 375° for 50–60 minutes. Bake *loaf* at 350° for 50–60 minutes or until toothpick inserted in center comes out clean. Frost as desired—chocolate was always my favorite!

YIELD: *1 loaf or 1 9-inch layer cake*

Grandma Nelson's Nisua

Nisua is a traditional Finnish bread that my friend Gail Bilto's grandmother perfected over many years. She varied the basic ingredients especially to please her granddaughters, Gail and Edwina. Grandma Nelson would get up at 3 A.M. so that by 8 A.M. the wonderful smell of fresh baked bread would awaken the girls.

The difficult task of getting Grandma's recipe on paper was accomplished by Edwina, who literally followed her around one morning, measuring each of the ingredients Grandma added only by instinct. This recipe is one to be treasured and the results will delight you.

Ingredients:

2 cups milk
2 tablespoons butter
1½ cups sugar
2 ¼-ounce envelopes dry yeast
9 cups unbleached all purpose flour (approximate)
4 large eggs at room temperature

20 cardamom pods (hulled and seeds ground, or 2 teaspoons ground)
1 teaspoon salt
2 tablespoons butter for final kneading

GLAZE:

1 egg
1 teaspoon milk

4 tablespoons coarsely granulated sugar

1. Heat milk and butter in 1-quart saucepan over medium heat until butter melts. Pour into large bowl, stir in 1 tablespoon of the sugar and allow milk mixture to cool to about 110° F. Stir in yeast to dissolve.
2. Whisk 3 cups of the flour into the yeast mixture. It will make a *thin* batter. Cover and proof in a warm, draft-free place until doubled in volume and spongy-looking, about 30 minutes to 1 hour.
3. While yeast is proofing, break eggs into a 1-quart bowl. Beat until frothy. Gradually add sugar, beating until mixture is thick and lemon-colored and sugar is dissolved. Beat in cardamom and salt.
4. When yeast mixture has doubled in bulk, stir in egg and sugar mixture.
5. Since most processors will not accommodate this amount of dough, do it in two batches. With steel blade in place, add 3 cups of the remaining flour to the work bowl. Cover and sift by processing for 3–4 on/off bursts. Turn processor on and pour half the yeast mixture through the feed tube. (There should be about 8 cups of the yeast mixture. Use a 1-cup measuring cup to facilitate pouring it into the feed tube.)
6. After half the yeast mixture has been added, continue processing until the dough forms a ball around the center shaft. Process 5 seconds more. Stop machine and remove cover. Press finger into dough. If it feels at all hard at center of dough, cover and process 5 seconds longer. Remove dough to lightly oiled bowl. Repeat with remaining 3 cups

flour and other half of yeast mixture. Add second ball of dough to another oiled bowl.

7. Dust work surface with ¼ cup flour. Rub hands with some of the butter for final kneading. Press the two balls of dough together. Place on floured work surface and knead together briefly. The secret to Grandma Nelson's Nisua is its fine satiny texture, which is the result of perfect kneading. The processor has done 99 percent of the job. Knead by hand until the dough does not stick to hands at all. (Add a bit more butter to your hands as necessary.) When dough is perfectly kneaded, place in large, lightly oiled bowl. Turn dough once to coat with oil. Cover and place in a warm, draft-free place until doubled in volume, about 1½–2 hours.

8. Punch down dough and let rest 10 minutes. Divide into 6 equal parts. Roll each piece into a long thin rope—about 1 inch in diameter. Pinch end of 3 ropes together and braid the ropes. Pinch other end. Tuck ends under and place braid on lightly oiled 12 x 17-inch baking sheet. Repeat with remaining three ropes. Cover loosely and let rise in a warm draft-free place until doubled in volume, about 1½ hours.

9. Preheat oven to 350°. Place rack in middle of oven. When braids have risen, beat egg lightly with milk for glaze and brush over braids, making sure glaze runs down into all crevices of braids. Sprinkle braids with coarsely granulated sugar.

10. Bake at 350° for 45 minutes to 1 hour until braids are golden brown and sound hollow when tapped on the bottom. Cool 10 minutes in pans and then remove to racks to cool completely.

YIELD: *2 braids*

Dear Friends,

I hope by now your food processor has become one of your favorite helpers in the kitchen. The possibilities for it are endless and through the years your creativity can take you well beyond the recipes here. All of the books included in my "New Age Kitchen Series"—of which this is the first—focus on how to get the most out of the amazing appliances now available and how to create a healthy, delicious cuisine with them.

I hope they serve you well!

All the best,

Annette Annechild

Annette Annechild

INDEX